SOME ENCHANTED EVENING
(A Song from the old musical South Pacific)

> Some enchanted evening
> You might see a stranger
> You might see a stranger
> Across a room full of people
> And something inside you
> Will clearly know
> That a bond between you
> Will grow and grow.
>
> Who can explain this?
> No one can tell you why!
> Fools might give you reasons,
> But the wise won't even try
>
> So fly to her/his side
> And make your love known
> Or for the rest of your life
> You might dream all alone

I have taken the liberty to paraphrase some of the words from the song "Some Enchanted Evening" from the famous 1958 Musical film, SOUTH PACIFIC (It costs a small fortune to quote even one line of a famous song). I guess for me it is one of the best expressions of "Soul Mate seeking" or "incurable romanticism" that I know.

There is clearly here a belief in love at first sight, at the instant knowing of one's future beautiful blissful bond with a person ostensibly a stranger, yet, strangely, already intimately known, and destined to be with you till death parts you two great lovers.

If you are a Soul Mate seeker or incurable romantic who can identify with the feelings expressed here, this book gives you a different perspective on all such deep impulses within you.

THE

SOUL MATE ILLUSION

First Edition

Published 2018 by Aron Gersh

at
Amazon.com

Human Potential Press

ISBN NUMBER
0-9516117-4-7 978-0-9516117-4-6

What This Book is About

The Soul Mate illusion is about how some of our infantile emotional needs still live on powerfully in adult falling in love. And there they create the illusion of a magical, mystical bond. However, this bond fails to see the full reality of the other person and of the situation. This reality, as we all know, will be seen later, when the romantic period comes to an end.

Generally, falling in love is honoured as a great and wonderful thing, unproblematic in itself, but leading to problems or "issues" later. All of this is well known.

What distinguishes the present book is this.I am suggesting that the problems of love do not merely come *later*, but are *already present* in the romantic period. These are problems which few want to look at. Because, after all, who wants to question feelings of blissful bonding?

The Soul Mate Illusion invites and challenges you to take a look at those problems, to interrogate the early bliss of falling in love. But please note that this book not cynical about love. What it aims to do is simply to suggest that "true love" must contain both "truth" and "love".

In short, what it suggests is that the misperception and fantasies of incipient romantic love, of Soul-mate-seeking, and of Soul Mate-finding arise from a *regressed* form of love which is *blind to reality*.

After all, doesn't real love imply a real connection with a real other?

People don't want to hear the truth,
because they don't want their
illusions destroyed
— Friederich Nietzche
(attributed)

RICHARD BACH'S "A BRIDGE ACROSS FOREVER"

There is also an Addendum at the back of the book giving an analysis of the famous Richard Bach/Leslie Parish Soul Mate relationship.
Richard Bach is the multi-best selling author of *Jonathan Livingstone Seagull*, *A Bridge across Forever* and other books.
The couple famously declared their relationship as a great Soul Mate relationship, and *A Bridge across Forever* was the story about how Richard found his Soul Mate Leslie. They toured America suggesting that there was no question they could not answer about Soul Mates. About 20 years later they were divorced, as good friends.
In a chapter at the end of this book I suggest some counter-points to the ideas they propounded on the nature of Soul Mates, based on the ideas of this book.

THREE EXAMPLE EXTRACTS FROM THIS BOOK

1

I have seen this phenomenon of romantic illusion both in my own youth, and in the lives of many others. Without exception, it goes like this:

When new love is blossoming, in all my dreams and visions my partner shares with me all the things of my life, and becomes part of my community. My partner will come with me to all the sporting events I go to, will enjoy all my friends, will come to all my presentations at my local groups, will allow me to share with her/him my excitement about the stories I hear, or that play out in operas, or in the books I read, etc. etc. Most importantly, my partner will delight in all the sweet, cute things I do, all the unique eccentricities I am.

However, in my dreams and visions, do I do the same for my partner? On the contrary, I seldom imagine myself loving my partner's eccentricities. I seldom imagine that she/he dreams of how I will be a big part of her life, her friends, and her family. (In truth, her interests, her friends and her family will probably bore me to tears! And when that becomes evident, then my partner's fantasies about me being his/her perfect partner will be shattered.)

While writing, I have just remembered an even younger vision of how I believed love should look. I think I was in my mid-teens. My inner image of "The Girl", "The One", "The True Love" was of some delightful-looking creature in the *background* of my life, my hobbies, my interests, my homework, or whatever. And there she was doing absolutely nothing herself, *except* to delight in what *I* was doing. Her function was simply to give me total attention, love and appreciation for all the things in my life that *I* was engaged with — very similar, in fact, to when I was a child, with my mum in viewing distance, and ready to be asked for appreciation by me for any mediocre achievement of mine!

In other words, "The Girl" in that inner image was just like "Good Mum". She was merely an "appreciation machine", with no tasks of her *own*, and with no need to seek appreciation for herself. All she needed in order to make me love her was her extreme physical attractiveness and her deep appreciation for me. Apart from that, she had little purpose.

Hmmm. Would she have bored me as I grew to a wise young age! (Well, even when I was young, a few minor parts of me were indeed wise!)

2

Respecting Values Which Are Totally Different From Mine

In this situation, we can truly say "we do not have this in common. Here, we do not complement each other. Neither are we the same, in this regard".

For example: I like holding on to objects found or bought which I consider to be sacred objects in my life, perhaps objects I find incredibly beautiful, or incredibly meaningful, or which hold important memories. These things are sacred to me. The past holds a vital background against which my present and future is figure, from which it is "projected" forward.

My partner is the opposite of me. We have nothing in common on this score. We are not the same, neither do our different ways complement each other. Our different ways clash completely —certainly in the living spaces which we share together. My partner believes in holding onto absolutely nothing. For her, sacredness consists of letting go of all and any such attachments, and moving on, beyond the past, beyond memories. For her, memories are just "sentimentality".

In such a situation partners can either totally and continually judge each other as "wrong", as "stupid" *or* can come to understand the validity of the other point of view, that the other side is as valid and in need of respect as our own viewpoint.

If my partner destroys something of mine because she thinks "it is stupid to hold onto things so preciously", she will be disrespecting my values. If I plead with her not to get rid of something that I think is important for her, but she insists, I might be failing to see how the world looks from *her* side.

Part of learning mature love, which is about going beyond narcissism, involves being able to listen very carefully to how my partner came to have that particular viewpoint, and how I, if I had walked the same path, in the same moccassins, would have come to the same conclusion.

This is a *skill* that must be learned, practised, developed, in order to be a better lover. It means learning to delight in or at least appreciate a difference which does not enhance one's own standpoint. And often, by understanding how your partner came to his or her point of view, you might even decide to change your own stance and values. Such good listening ability leads to something called 'growing and changing'. And we might note how easily and often we meet people with whom we have a lot in common, but we do not feel desire to have intimate love with them. This is to say, just because "we have so much in common", this does not mean we will love and delight in each other.

3

A SENSE OF BOUNDARY-LESS-NESS

"We are One"

Accompanying dependence and narcissism in romantic lovers is a sense of no boundary between thee and me: I don't know where I end and you begin, where you begin and I end; we are one; we are merged, in bliss.

Similarly, for the early infant, there is no sense of a boundary separating it and mother, and it and the world. In fact, for the baby, mother *is* the whole world. This begins right in the womb, where we experience a floating, "oceanic" boundaryless state in which there is no difference between our insides and our outsides.

Once we are born and (with any luck) start breast-feeding, we experience a similar bond with mother. There is no sense of "me and mother" for the early infant. Like Soul Mates, we are "One". It does not even make sense to describe us as "Us" — there is no "Us". My whole young world is simply one quagmire of sensations. I experience no boundary between myself and mother. For all intents and purposes now, mother is the whole world. There is only "One". (101)

Of course, when the infant feels good, *the real reason* is that it has been well nurtured all round. But it is possible for the infant to have painful, inner, "growth pains" not caused by a lack of nurturing. Whether the infant's pain or pleasure is generated from itself or from mother, it is all experienced as "one". So when "I" feel displeasure, for whatever cause, (my self, or mother), it is both myself and "the world" which is in a bad, dis-pleasurable state. There is no world that exists outside of my inner state (which is projected outside of my skin to "the world", which is basically mother) and no inner state that does not speak of the state of "the world".

When there is happiness, there is happiness all round. When there is pain, all the world, me, and mother are in pain, though the infant does not distinguish between the three things. Because of this, there is no identifying of what causes what — or I should say of who is doing what to whom. Psychoanalysis talks of the baby's Omnipotent Fantasies —that it "thinks" it causes its needs to be met *simply by having them.*

Now, it is probably frustration of need which teaches the baby that there is a distinction between it and mother, and that its good feelings, as well as its bad, are caused mainly by what mother does for it. Frustration "teaches" the infant its boundaries, its separation from mother. Because of frustration, it slowly has to figure out who is doing what to whom — here realizing it is mum doing this to me. But of course before this realisation, there is not much sense of who is doing what to whom, because there really is no "who" and no "whom".

The main point to be made here is that sometimes Soul Mates and romantic lovers also speak of this "I don't know where he ends and I begin". They speak of being merged and they speak of not knowing quite who is doing what to whom. That is, they cannot locate cause and effect for the incredible bliss they feel.

But there is an element of regression operating here. I suggested that we should be aware of such powerful regressions in what appear to be "positive" relationships, such as Soul-mate-seekers and romantics seek and temporarily find. The narcissism I described suggested that we think that the *other's* needs are fulfilled automatically by their fulfilling *our* needs. Also, the emotional dependence that seemingly operates so satisfactorily, so nourishingly, helps with this sense of no-boundaries. This is part of the process of feeling as "One" — the perfect flow between needs needed and needs fulfilled help create the illusion of boundarylessness.

AUTHOR'S NOTE

THE SOUL MATE ILLUSION and *FALLING FOR LOVE*
This is a book with a fair smattering of ideas about what makes up "true love" and how we are easily fooled by love's illusions. Whether I have expressed these ideas comprehensibly or not, I would like to think that there are a few really useful sentences on the nature of love here which could be valuable for anyone.

The *Soul Mate Illusion* is a shorter version of my previous book, *Falling for Love*. That book is probably more suited for folk who have some knowledge, or interest in, the subject of psychology generally. I think too that students of psychology might have some benefit in terms of learning some psychology concepts there. The Soul Mate Illusion is, I hope more understandable by the general populace.

I think that *The Soul Mate Illusion* would certainly be enjoyed by those who like thinking deeply about things, those who apply difficult concepts to their own personal experiences in all the delights of love, as well as to its disappointments.

But let me repeat: *The Soul Mate Illusion* is in no wise cynical about love. Instead, it urges us towards a deeper, truer love than the illusory "true love" of the romantics.

It is certainly this author's wish that you keep this book on your (digital) shelf and re-read it a few times over a lifetime. I don't believe the ideas expressed here will ever be dated. Because of our on-going life experience of love, and also because of our (hopefully) greater openness to new ideas as we get older and realize how little we really know, I believe you will "get" different aspects of this book at different ages of your life. Different light bulbs will be lit in the inner room of your life experience at different stages of your life. We could and should all become better at being loving and at being lovers as we grow up and older. "Knowing now . . ." what we wish we had "known then", makes us potentially wiser in our loving *now*.

I also hope that you will read this book slowly, and thoughtfully. And you are welcome to send me any comments about areas where you think I am mistaken. Inevitably I have blind spots of my own. Please share with me any experiences you might want to share, relative to the ideas expressed here.

I have suggested herein that we should pause thoughtfully before "welcoming lovers", and be prepared to interrogate their fabulous happiness. I don't really know of another that has dedicated itself to putting such big question marks on the very blissful and delightful experience of falling in (sorry, *for*) love.

Then again, perhaps we should indeed "welcome lovers", as suggested by the hit song "As Time Goes By" from the movie *Casablanca* – but not, however, as two people who have reached the *final* stage of the long journey to love. Rather, we should honour them, (and indeed ourselves if it is us), for *beginning* a great journey of exploration, both into our partners, but also, indeed, into some of the deeper, challenged and challenging parts of ourselves. All who enter into a relationship take a brave leap into an adventure and a quest, and we should honour all as heroes.

Forgive me for not addressing gender issues. When writing about mother-child relationships, it is easier, for the sake of avoiding confusion, to assume the child is male.

Thanks for reading. I wish you Love and Truth, Authenticity and Personal Growth!

Aron Gersh, M.A.

TABLE OF CONTENTS

THE

SOUL MATE

ILLUSION

by

Aron Gersh

INTRODUCTORY

CHAPTERS

INTRODUCTION

The Soul Mate Illusion

Are you dying to meet your "Soul Mate", the "love of your life", the one you were "meant to be with forever", the one you would recognise at first sight and on the first meeting?

Pause a while!

This book suggests that you might be in the grip of a certain type of illusion. This author suggests that you interrogate the inner state that drives you to seek out that "perfect one meant for you forever".

But don't get me wrong. I am totally in favour of deep love, wonderful love, *real* love. In this book there is no cynicism about love. In fact, there is full encouragement to find the most appropriate partner, for the greater happiness and the greater good of both of you.

What this book proposes, however, is that there are certain "traps" that might initially *look* like love, which might *feel* deeply like love, which might convince you overwhelmingly of love. But all of these will turn out to be illusions which unravel as the reality of what is happening begins to appear. This is why the great and glittering fairy-tale romances soon consume themselves, leaving nothing but ashes. And this is not only true of famous media romances, but for the most ordinary of us.

In *The Soul Mate Illusion* I try to explain why this happens, and why and how it might be happening to *you*. At the end of the book I encourage you to seek wonderful *real* love, and to deal wisely and creatively with the love's illusions.

For the word "illusion" seems particularly apt. It makes me think of magicians performing magic tricks. Because, watching – not *observing* – the magician, we don't really know what is going on in the *background*. For that reason, what is happening seems to be happening magically, mysteriously.

But once we learn how the trick is done, once we learn what is *really* happening in the background, the magic disappears, and we would not spend one second wanting to watch that same trick. Our time can then be spent on solving real-life problems with hard-won, worked-on, creative solutions. And this is also a kind of magic. Magic of a higher, more *real* kind.

The Soul Mate Illusion, then, is trying to suggest to you what might be going on unconsciously, *behind the scenes* of romance. *The Soul Mate Illusion* is an attempt to explain some aspects of human psychology that many readers may not be aware of.

The difference to watching a magician is that in romantic love it is we ourselves who are producing the magic that we are watching – experiencing it with delight, but unable to see what is hidden from us: the real cause of the production of the magic. We can't see what we ourselves are secretly doing to produce the trick. So what are we doing?

We are misperceiving!

We are making something look like it is not!

That "something" is, firstly, our *lover*, the object of our love; and, secondly, the *nature of our connection* with her or him.

Now just how do you make something look like something it is not? Well, think of when we idealize/idolize a famous person. We might accurately see their wonderful qualities, but onto those we add *other* qualities they might not have – say, loyalty, trustworthiness, openness, honesty. Or even happiness, self-esteem, self-confidence and inner peace. In this way, our ideal and idolized heroes might well turn out to be murderers, or suicides, or partner-abusers, or addicts, or depressives, not feeling adequately loved despite all their public acclaim. And this also applies to the most ordinary of us.

Additionally, we might fail to see negative qualities which our heroes *do* in fact possess, perhaps because we are naïve, or because we are in denial. With experience, however, we get better at seeing what is there and also what is not there in another person, and we finally realize what we had formerly failed to see (negative qualities). The result is that we come to devalue persons we might at first have valued. Or, learning to see someone's positive qualities, we later come to value those we had formerly devalued.

But there is one process which is part of this magical misperception of another (and for the purpose of this book, of our lover). This is a process that is sometimes not so easily corrected by life experience. We have to be aware of it before we will see the trick —before we will correct our misperception. I am referring to the process where we *add on* qualities to our lover (or any other human being), qualities that really aren't there at all. In psychology, we call this process Projection — and in fact the image of a film projector *is* a good way to illustrate it. I'll get to this shortly.

The fifty-year period from roughly the 70's to the present seems to have been a period of prolific Soul-mate-seeking. Corresponding almost perfectly to the rise to the highest divorce rates in the West, Soul-mate-seeking seemed to originate from a craving in people for marriages or other unions which had "that something more" than what came and was expected from traditional marriages. That Soul-mate-seeking did not quite succeed in creating a high percentage of beautiful blissful bonds that last forever is easy enough to realize when we look around us. Relationships seem as difficult as ever, and marriage counsellors and relationship counsellors have proliferated, not to mention a host of relationship teachers, attempting to help the process along, the process towards relationships that can somehow be described as "successful". (My own subjective statistic about this is that I see about 2 - 3% of all relationships, married or otherwise, about which I would say "they are a successful couple! That is how good relationships ought to be".)

This book is suggesting that the idea of finding a Soul Mate, usually defined as some sort of perfect partner, is illusory. Indeed, it is noticeable how often the great romances, both of the rich and famous, and of the most ordinary of us, fall apart at the seams. Usually these are precisely the ones where the couples start out proclaiming that they have found their Soul Mate, their perfect-fit partner.

What goes wrong? How could something which seems so solid and beautiful and eternal switch quite suddenly into something ugly, conflict-ridden, and falling-apart-at-the-seams, something not destined for eternity at all? In short, how could people so easily have fallen *for* love?

Well, older and wiser folk, whether cynical or not, often know that a couple deeply and romantically in love will *wake up* from their "bliss-bunny" phase. Often, the older and wiser among us caution the individuals in that relationship not to make radical decisions in the "romantic phase" of a relationship — thus implicitly suggesting that later there will be a rather "un-romantic phase". The couple will then have to wake up to something called "reality" — when the wonderful, blissful romantic phase dies down, or is quickly killed off by two realizations:

One, that *conflict* is inherent in any and every relationship, a conflict which, if not handled creatively, can lead to alienation and perhaps even breakup. Differences which at first were delightful are replaced by differences not delighted in, causing conflict.

And two, that whatever is *childish* needs to be outgrown, so that the relationship ends up with two *adults* rather than with two *regressed* "*children*".

So far I am not telling you anything new. Remember: the problem period is popularly deemed to begin *after* the romantic period! No one regards the romantic period to be problematic in itself. And much has been written about this.

For instance, according to the 1931 song, *As Time Goes By*, made famous in the 1942 classic movie *Casablanca*:

The world will always welcome lovers,
as time goes by

And it is true. So many of us see excited new lovers, and let them cross the street before us. We hail them and honour them and delight in them, venerating what we see as a sacred union.

In this book, however, the sacredness and wonderfulness of the bliss-bunny romantic phase is called into question. It is suggested that perhaps there is a problem here already, here *in the romantic period*, and that we need to be aware of that too — not just to wait *for the later periods* which show up *their* problems.

In *The Soul Mate Illusion*, I discuss the problems *within* the romantic period itself. These are not problems that correct themselves spontaneously. They require in-sight from the lovers — the ability to see deeply *inside*!

17

The same applies to the beautiful blissful bond which Soul-Mate-Seekers might experience in the beginning of their relationship. The deep reverence lovers might experience at first in their amazing connection might possess elements that are worth putting into question, worth examining under a microscope. It is precisely this and mainly this problem that is addressed in this book. Thousands of other books on intimate love deal with the issues that happen at the end of the romantic phase – the bliss-bunny phase. Then reality strikes, and conflict and disappointment begin.

I believe *The Soul Mate Illusion* is unique in suggesting we need to take a deeper look at the period that seems so unproblematic, the romantic phase. Because this phase is so pleasurable and joyful, who would want to question it? But if we saw an ecstatically happy person who was drunk, or on drugs, or a manic-depressive (bipolar) person in their manic phase, we would immediately question the reality of their happiness. In a similar way, I am asking you to question the reality of Soul Mate and romantic joy — but not in order to be a killjoy! Rather, in order to change love into "realjoy".

PROJECTION - THE MAGIC OF NOT SEEING CLEARLY

Earlier, I said there is one process of magical misperception that is not spontaneously corrected by life experience, a process requiring psychological knowledge in order to be able to see the trick. This is the process of Projection, and I suggested that the film projector is an excellent way to illustrate how it works.

A film projector "throws" an image onto a blank screen. Till it does so, there is nothing but the blank screen. When it does so, a clear picture emerges on the screen, where it seems to exist so powerfully. But of course the picture is actually generated from inside the projector, and at first exists there and only there.

Similarly, when we project onto others an image that does not inherently belong to them, it means we have that image inside ourselves, and we "throw it" onto the "blank screen" of another's skin, another's being, thus creating an amazing magic trick. A trick involving of course, a false perception of the other's true nature, "putting things onto the other" that aren't really there.

There has been a widespread tendency, at least in some circles in the psychological professions, to suggest that projection means that "if we see some quality in another, this means the very same quality has to be in *ourselves*". This idea also has found widespread usage in general Western society: "If you think *I* am a cheat (or selfish, or angry, etc. etc.) it means that *you* are a cheat (or selfish, angry, etc. etc.). In other words, point a finger at *me* about X and it means that three other fingers are pointing back at *you* about the same thing, that same X quality.

On behalf of the psychological establishment, this author squirms with shame at such a stupid, simplistic and inaccurate idea from a discipline that has produced so many great insights. My usual rough-and-ready response is that "the lion knows that it must chase and eat a buck, not because it *is* a buck or has a buck *inside* itself, but because it is capable of recognising something totally *other* than itself — a buck". It is absurd to tell the lion: "because you *see* a buck, you must *be* a buck yourself, or have 'buckness' *inside* you".

Of course this is not to deny that there *are* occasions in human interaction where such a projective phenomenon *does* occur — where what we see in others is not in *them* but in *us* (for example, when a man repressing his own homosexuality sees homosexuality in fully heterosexual males, failing to see it in himself). This form of projection, however, is of a rarer kind.

So how does it work that we can "ascribe some quality to another that is actually generated from within us, and is not an accurate description of them at all, but neither is it a quality of ourselves"?

> **The less defined, the less clearly visible, the less seen of the thing we are looking at, the more we are able to project onto it.**

Here is how.

Just because we are carrying something *inside* ourselves, it does not mean that it is *about* ourselves.

From our earliest years, we take into our consciousness (our "minds"), images of the natures and qualities of all others we relate to. Together with an *image* of them go images of our *relationships* with them — the way we think about them, feel about them, react to who they are, and have intuitions about them. Hence what is inside us is not just our own qualities and/or images of our qualities, but also a whole catalogue of images of others — including our images of how we personally relate to them, because of *our* qualities. For instance, being very sensitive around someone whom we see as "insensitive".

Because we have such an array of images of others, it is possible to project onto others in such a way that what we are seeing in them is not really *in* them, is put *onto* them by us. But I repeat: these needn't necessarily be qualities of ourselves. Thus I am able to project an image of my mother onto my wife, to react to her *as if* she were my mother, even when that quality of my mother is not at all in my wife, or, *for that matter, in me.* What I *do* possess is an inner image of my mother, and I am capable of projecting that onto my wife.

There is one aspect of projection, this widespread phenomenon of misperception, that is worth noting. The less defined, the less clearly visible, the less seen of the thing we are looking at, the more we are able to project onto it. *The vaguer the stimulus, the easier the projection* — the more we are able to *"image-in"* something that is there that is not. The more defined and clear is the thing we are perceiving, the less likely it is that can "put on it" something from within us that contradicts what we so clearly see. Clear vision in love and in life means realising our projections, and coming to see that is what is going on with others in the world is not what we originally thought it was — is not what we *projected* it to be.

What is the relevance of this for "the Soul Mate illusion"?

The relevance is that human beings are very complex: it is impossible to get a clear picture of a person instantly or in a short amount of time. We need time if we are to unfold to each other, to show each other who we really are, in many different contexts. This is all to say that when we hardly know someone, in the early days of our meeting them, they are precisely the vague, undefined "stimulus" most favourable to projection.

The picture we have of them is rather sketchy, and there are many blank parts too. This allows for us to project an enormous amount onto them, most of which is likely to be an inaccurate perception of them, a wrong "guess" as to how they will behave in certain situations. Therefore, in newly formed relationships, Soul-Mate-Seekers and incurable romantics should always bear in mind the possibility of major misperception.

But here's the rub: at the time of falling in love, who wants to express doubt, to spoil the current beautiful bliss?

WORDS FOR LOVE FROM THE ANCIENT GREEKS AND ROMANS

I'd like to introduce here some of the useful terms the ancient Greeks and Romans had for love, and will refer to them throughout the book.

Firstly, there was *Ludus*, which referred to playful love. Arguably, playfulness is a thing we bring from childhood, a childlike thing, more than an adult thing.

Secondly, there was *Eros*, which is about erotic love. It can also refer to simply being "turned on" by another's strengths and potentials, in the less sexy domains.

Thirdly, there was *Pragma* (related to the word "pragmatic"), which refers to adult, practical love. Being a "practical couple" might mean we fail to be erotic and playful – but hopefully not.

Philos can, very roughly be considered here to mean "friendly" (but not erotic) love — that sort of feeling of warm, fuzzy love for a good friend. It includes support for another when they are weak, wounded and in pain, etc. The word "philanthropy", literally translated, mean "love of humans".

Fourthly, there is *Philautia*, which referred to love of one's self — not to be confused with selfishness or narcissism.

Fifthly, there is *Agape*, which refers to "Brotherly love" or "Christian love" or "Fellowship love"

I would suggest that the popular form of romantic love, the one we all rave and dance about and whose seeming great joy we celebrate, is mainly a mix of Ludus and Eros, playfulness of all kinds, including erotic playfulness. I am saying that this popular version we rave about is mainly a childhood sort of thing, with lots of childlike playfulness in it.

But there is also a less popular, less playful, less flamboyant form of romantic love, where the bond is formed by the *healing* of each other's childhood wounds, insecurities, inadequacies, and so on — when two "lonely" people get together.

In both cases, the suggestion is that romantic love is mostly and mainly a *childhood* sort of experience. We might say it is a "regressive" experience.

End of Introduction

21

FALLING IN LOVE

—*The Great Pleasurable Overreaction*

Our projections may or may not be moderated by life experience. When they are, we realise "we were blind, but now we see" — an amazing grace of insight into our previous illusions. The "images collection" relating to the look and natures of others which we carry around within us, although it develops mainly in our earliest childhood years, is added to by all our life experiences until early adulthood. By that time we have a fairly stable view of the world and its people, a whole collection of "videos" that we can play on others' bodies, on others' beings.

Now here is the central thesis of this book: The most powerful adult projective images arise in our earliest infancy in relation to our mother, and thus to a powerful, intimate bonding situation. It is precisely these images which are projected onto, added onto – what we *think* we are seeing in our new lover. After all, falling in love is once again seeking a powerful bonding situation with another human being.

We can talk of three classes of Early Infantile Experience with the mother. From her we get:

1. good nurturance, and the fulfilment of our needs;
2. bliss, comfort, safety and security;
3. love and attention.

Inevitably, there are some gaps in our nurturance. Some are temporary, but some are more permanent, where our parents may fail to recognise a major need which should be fulfilled for a baby, but which they did not. This leaves feelings of "holes" in us, leaves us feeling "less than whole". Sins of omission.

On the other hand, some mothers (and fathers too) may deliberately do things which traumatize us as young infants, leaving wounds, and the scars of wounds, in us. Sins of commission.

Now Soul-mate-seekers and Incurable Romantics long to recreate that primal state, the state of perfect bliss with mother when our needs were effortlessly fulfilled in infancy and in the womb. This gives rise to the most ideal form of the projection, and of the desire for a perfect fit, for a beautiful blissful bond with one's partner.

All the same, because there are inevitably gaps in mother's nurturance, no matter how good her intentions, we are always left with some unsatisfied needs. Consequently, we may hope for and seek for a partner who can fulfil *all* of our primal needs, *including* the ones that mother was unable to fulfil.

If, however, we have been wounded in infancy by some form of abuse, we may hope for and seek a partner who is the perfect healer.

Accordingly, the Soul Mate illusion consists in not being aware that what we may be seeking and hoping for, or what we have found when we think we have found perfection, is merely a *projection* of feelings and inner states which stem from our connection with mother from the womb right up to our second year – a time before we can use words to describe what is in us, what we are experiencing.

Soul Mate relationships are seen as relationships with some perfect kind of blissful bond. The images of "true love" which Incurable Romantics project are also hooked on the great bliss to be found. The thesis of this book is that this need (when one is still alone) or this fantasy, this illusion (when one feels one has found one's perfect fit) is a recreation of one's early infant state of bliss with mother, before one could even talk. In other words, this book is suggesting that when we fall in (sorry, for) love, we are projecting.

So, although a perfect fit may involve all three classes of early experience, we will be concentrating on the first one: good nurturance, and the fulfilment of our needs. But we will also keep in mind the other two classes of infantile experience — the sense of wanting to find a perfect "fulfiller of our unfulfilled experiences" and also a perfect "healer of our childhood wounds".

The suggestion is that all three of these classes of experience create illusions in loving intimacy, and all must be surpassed, left behind, grown out of, if we are to become adults capable of real true love, of true real love. I repeat: We have to *see* the illusions, and *surpass* them.

> **Regressive feelings are very powerful, create great blissful excitement, but blind us to the reality of what is before us.**

Nevertheless, it is only fair to acknowledge that not all thinkers in psychology would agree with me. Some suggest that the perfect times of bonding with mother form a *healthy and desirable pattern* to strive for in adult relationships — that, if we have *lost* that beautiful bonding sense, we should try and recapture it, in order to create the best possible adult bond with someone. The suggestion from those theorists is that in growing up, we lost valuable knowledge and impulses from infancy and childhood years, and that we would do well to re-find those, for they are deemed to hold the best patterns for adult life. Their view, *unlike the view of this book*, is that those early blissful experiences recreated in adult life equate to a great adult bonding experience. As will become clear, I believe this to be a mistake.

A number of things need be said about my central thesis.

I am talking about the bonding in the period of early infancy that goes up to about two years of age, i.e. before the infant can talk, and is just getting more mobile. The powerful bonding of those years takes place when infants have no words to describe their inner feelings or state of being.

Indeed, the Latin root of the word "infant" literally means "unable to speak". Later it will be able to say "that is nice" or "not nice". But not yet. Thus, it has no words to describe the perfect bonding time of that period, or with which to describe a perfect bonding never experienced. And later, in adult years, when such bliss *is* captured in falling in love, it is often described as "ineffable" — i.e., "words cannot describe it!"

Projections are based on *needs and fears*. So in the case of Soul-mate-seeking, it is a deep *need* for perfect bonding. Once attained, there might be *fear* of its splitting apart. We can hear this in the many songs about passionate love which sing of the fear that the lover will go away, or somehow break the bond. Songs of loss and of betrayal.

There is a growing body of evidence that our visions of the world (our image of things outside of us, things that are "not-us") begins right in the womb. The plethora of experiences one has in the womb already give us some kind of picture both of the nature of our mother, and also what we "think" is "the world generally" — is it a kind place or a cruel place? Is it peaceful or turbulent or healthily nourishing or challengingly poisonous? Is it abundant or depriving?

Precisely because these experiences in the womb, followed by our infantile experiences are pre-verbal, *they are also not easily identifiable as happening in adult life.* This is utterly different from having a bad experience with, say, a certain kind of person, or animal, when one is five years old or so – i.e., in the *post-*verbal stage – and therefore knowing, from memory, *and being able to formulate in words,* why one might mistrust such a person or animal.

That is to say, for our post-infancy experiences, we can easily discover the source of our projections, and have insight into their origins. For instance, when a spouse reacts strongly to a partner each time the partner is seen to disappoint in some way, a therapist might ask: "Who does that remind you of in your childhood?". And in most cases there is a quick and easy answer. The spouse realises that he is acting towards his partner as if she were one of his parents.

Very often, it is when someone *overreacts* to something done or said by another, that we have evidence of regression — they are seeing the present as if it is a rehash of some past event, usually with mother or father or other carers or siblings. (Not all strong reactions are necessarily overreactions, but many are. This is discussed in much more depth in my other book, *Falling for Love*).

It is relatively easy to find the origins of projections from periods in our lives which can be recaptured in memory. Usually they are specific and unique experiences, and they go back only to about four years of age. Also, they are specific to that individual, not generalised aspects of growing up: "My father threw me into the swimming pool before I knew how to swim", etc.

This is not to deny that there are unique and specific experiences in the early post-verbal period. There are, especially with mother. But in this book I shall not be touching on these. Rather, I concentrate on aspects of the mother-baby relationship which are universal, common to all of us, and hence, theoretically, should also transcend culture. I will suggest seven of these aspects of. I call them *Elements Of Regression*.

Before I get to that, I would like to point out that most couple's therapists who "go back in time to early childhood relationships with mother and father" generally only go back as far as to three or four years of age. In other words, the assumption is that what happened *before* that age has no effect, is a blank slate. I think there is a serious gap in theory here that needs correcting, in spite of all the good work and successes of good couple's therapists like Harville Hendrix and his wife and colleague Helen LaKelly Hunt.

The term "overreaction" – for instance, oversensitivity to benign comments – when seen as a sign of regression, is generally used about painful or embarrassing and generally unpleasant, "negative" things. The thesis of this book, on the other hand, is that romantic love is the great *"positive"* and *pleasurable* overreaction. One is reacting with more intense *pleasure* than the situation actually warrants.

End of Love as the great overreaction

ELEMENTS

OF

REGRESSION

ELEMENTS OF REGRESSION

Reliving the Past

> These Seven elements of regression constitute the greater part of the glue which binds new lovers blissfully together.

INTRODUCING THE ELEMENTS OF REGRESSION

So, you are falling in love with a Soul Mate, or you are wanting to, seeking out him or her, you are waiting for their mysterious magical appearance. If you are falling in love it means that until now all potential partners you met created in you a mixed feeling (generally known as "ambivalence") and you were not sure at all of them. But now, suddenly, the mixed feelings are gone.

What happens when we fall in (sorry, *for*) love, is that our ambivalence disappears and is replaced by certainty. The glue that now binds you to this person might very well flow from the re-creation of that state, or that expectation, of the childhood bliss you either had or had lost out on. You are in a primitive infantile state which feels like a "beautiful blissful bond". It is a projection of "good mother" onto our partner, seeing not only the real good in them, but pasting some extra indescribable goodies onto them that are not really there. The re-creation is a *feeling* state! A *feeling* about the nature of our *bond*!

This is not to say there is not a substantial vision of an adult connection you have with this person. You accurately see many parts of both of your adult lives which mesh with each other — either because you are the same, or because you complement each other. He likes to eat a lot; you like to cook a lot. You are a dancer; he is a musician. You are a business woman, a trader; he is good at bookkeeping and money management; you both like hiking and camping, and so on.

But hidden within this apparently adult blissful non-ambivalence is also the projection, the re-creation of pure infantile bliss. You are unconscious of the deeper processes going on here, sustaining the magic, thus producing the illusion that at last you are in a state of non-ambivalent bliss, certain of your love. It is a re-creation of feelings! It is a *fantasy* of having no more mixed feelings!

I have suggested that the infantile part of this state of non-ambivalence in romantic love and Soul-mate-seeking is a parallel with our early bond with mother at its best. When we are born, there is almost universally "love at first sight" by mothers for their newborn babies. There is a deep recognition of the uniqueness of this baby, and mother and baby can uniquely identify each other by the tiniest of parameters, like smell and "feel". There is also a sense, especially for the baby, of there being no boundaries between it and mum.

Experiences such as these appear to be similar to adult experiences of falling in love, especially when there is that deep sense of "we were made for each other, destined for each other", of being "a perfect fit".

As long as you understand how we often see the world in a symbolic way, you will be able to understand how we tend to see our partner *as if* she or he is our "good mother", or at least, similar to those aspects of our mother which we perceived as infants. (Note that, for the purposes of this book, I am dealing with the *very strongest and earliest* bond issues, and so do not include father-bonding here.)

NO WORDS TO DESCRIBE SUCH WONDERFUL FEELINGS!

The earliest experiences we have, happen at a time when we have no language, and we have lots of fairly passive physical contact as our main communication with our mother. One good definition of a baby is "a relationship to a mother". When we say a baby is a relationship to a mother, this means that the pattern from here that is "re-membered" (put together again) in later life contains both a sense of yourself plus an image of your mother and an inextricable relationship of some kind or other between the two of you as one. Mother, in our earliest months, is a powerful yet unutterable, ineffable, indescribable sense of a being who has powerfully but mysteriously acted as our host — but who has no name, no as-yet-identified separate identity. She exists as a kind of phantom, a chimera — a wispy, transparent ghost of an image. But an incredibly powerful one.

Being fairly passive during infancy, we are subject to many passions — being "moved" emotionally and physically, from joy to temporary separation, from longing to bliss, and so forth.

Is this beginning to sound like some people's image of their partner in the early romantic phases? For the bliss of romantic love is mysterious, often can't easily be described, sees the lover as some kind of wispy phantom, and the power of that phantom subjects us to many passions.

It is my contention that the extremely mysterious joys and fears of the early part of the romantic phase of relationships is a reliving of the pre-verbal bonding period. We recreate, in adult life, an inner feeling of well-being, and project a quality of nurturance onto our partner, just as the blissful baby feels toward a splendidly nurturing mother. We successfully recreate this, or implicitly seek to recreate it, hope for it, or expect it, in later adult romantic love. These recreations of the past in the present are called *regressions*.

This early childhood bonding experience re-created in romantic love has a number of qualities which I call "Elements of Regression", of which identify at least seven. When we think we have found our Soul Mate partner, or are in the romantic phase of a relationship, my contention is that it is worth trying to become conscious of whether any of these regressions are operating in us, or in our partner. And we may be acting as loyal and valued friends if we can help others in what one might call "regressed romances" to see what they might be doing.

So here, dear Reader, is where I am asking you to take up the challenge of *The Soul Mate Illusion* — especially if you yourself are a Soul-Mate-*Seeker* or an *Incurable Romantic*. Read each one of these "elements of regression", let them seep into your soul, and subtly feel out if they seem to make any sense to you — either in relation to your existing Soul Mate relationship, or to your images of the one you are searching for.

As you read, see if something about these elements "clicks". You may feel that only some, not all, apply to your loving situation. But I believe that the vast majority of us will find some recognition of ourselves here, and hence some value in all of this.

End of Intro to Elements of Regression

LOVE AT FIRST SIGHT

Instant recognition of our special bond

Because Soul-Mate-Seekers tend to believe that their Soul Mate was known in a past life, they assume there will be an instant recognition when they meet again in this life. They would "just know" magically, that they belong, uniquely, together, because they would remember each other from a past incarnation. There would thus be "love at first sight". They would know, magically, that they are to create the beautiful blissful connection which only they have together, the perfect fit.

Surprisingly enough, there is an early-life situation which has very similar elements.

> "I believe in love at first sight, because the moment I was born, I fell in love with my mother

Someone posted this quote on the internet:

> *I believe in love at first sight, because the moment I was born, I fell in love with my mother.*

> "This relationship was meant to be"
> "We were meant for each other"
> "You are my destiny"

Indeed, first *sight* of mother came soon after birth. But first *experience* of mother begins right in the womb. There, mother and I have a profound and complex symbiotic relationship. I tell her I need to eat spinach and chocolates, and I make her crave those. She forces too spicy curry into me. It's in the amniotic fluid, and I get to taste it because my taste buds are functioning already.

I don't like it much, but I get used to it, and I certainly get to know it. Her voice and her unique language and dialect vibrate through her body and into me. Nobody else can hear my mother's voice in this unique and muffled way. I also hear the dialogue of the soap operas she watches, and the music she listens to.

It has been proven (read Ann Murphy Paul's book "Origins" ref.) that after birth the baby can recognise these sounds, and these tastes, and the mother's voice, and so on, which were all there before birth.

Did I say "recognise"?

Yes, I did!

And instantly!

Isn't this beginning to sound a bit like the Soul-Mate-seekers talking about instant recognition of the one they are *supposed* to be with? Doesn't the baby's recognition of a "past life" in the womb" sound like the Soul-Mate-seeker's belief in knowing the person they are about to bond with "from a past life", with an instant recognition?

The deep connectedness formed between the foetus in mother's womb and mother herself is rediscovered again after birth. Baby knows and loves mother's voice, smell and so on, more than anyone else's. Clearly, this must be a feeling of "this relationship is meant to be", a feeling of "we were meant for each other", a sense of "you are my destiny" — just in the same way that those who feel they have found their Soul Mate have found the bond *they* are meant to be in.

Consequently, this is the unique being with whom unique me has to be bonded.

Here the special bond is to occur.

Here I am to receive untold pleasure and comfort.

Here I shall receive all the nourishment I need in order to grow and develop.

Here all my pains will be healed and transformed into comfort again.

And here, if my pains cannot be healed, is where they are meant to be suffered.

In the adult romantic arena, the magical connection discovered between unique mother and unique me translates as "love at first sight".

I suggest that this pattern of instant recognition which is associated with a deep sense of the total "appropriateness" of this bond, no matter how pleasurable or painful, sets us up to seek a similar perfect bond as adults. Soul-Mate-Seekers who claim to have found their Soul Mates talk of "coming home at last"

As grownups, we cannot live the lives of infants.

I will later suggest, instead, that in fact growing up means "*leaving* home".

Our universal regressive need to fall in love this way, by an instant recognition of extreme uniqueness, is brilliantly used by scriptwriters of Hollywood movies to bring us to tears. (Even the present author is not immune.) We are deeply touched by seeing such love being simplistically enacted in a movie story which lasts for just 2 hours.

Nowhere is this belief in the magic of finding one's unique partner, and knowing them instantly, better portrayed than in the movie *Sleepless in Seattle*. This is probably one of a few romantic stories where the heroine (played by Meg Ryan) and hero (played by Tom Hanks) never meet until the very end of the story, and then presumably "live happily ever after". (Naturally, the romantic story teller does not wish to tell the real story about the later discovery of ambivalence, and the difficulty of dealing with real-world issues, and real-world relationships.)

In that movie, the couple know all along – though based on the flimsiest knowledge of each other – that they are "destined to be together", that they were "meant for each other". I showed, when discussing the phenomenon on projection, that it works best when what we are projecting onto is an ambiguous or even vague stimulus. And that is precisely what we have in this movie: two people who have a rather vague knowledge of each other based on the smallest bytes of information. Their take on each other is motivated, I suggest, by the regressive fantasy of a magical connection to a unique bonding partner. A partner who is called – wait for it, and cue drum roll – ... "Mother"!

Of course, we ourselves might fall in love this way, by an instant, magical, unique recognition of another who shall be our partner from henceforth and forever more. But this is a total regression to a childhood state. It is effectively an illusion, because, while as the young of a species may "know" mother perfectly, and magically, *as grownups we cannot form attachments as easily*.

As complex grownup creatures, we cannot live the lives of infants. Yet the fantasy of that perfect fit, that unique bond happening magically, is an unconscious attempt to live the infantile love which has been wrongly identified as a perfectly adult form of life.
It is a whole world of needs fulfilled, of wounds healed – a whole world *projected or painted* onto a canvas that has only the first of many visible brushstrokes upon it.

End of Love at First Sight

THE MAGIC OF SPECIAL UNIQUENESS

Soul-Mate-seekers who have recently *found* their Soul Mate generally describe the relationship as magical. There is magic in the connection, magic in all need-fulfilment, magic even in conflict resolution and reconciliation. Needs seem to be satisfied magically by the other, and conflict is resolved magically by brilliant communication and instantly occurring forgiveness about any arising "differences". Pain is soon healed.

For those still *seeking* their Soul Mate relationship, the *expectation* will be that the connection will be magical, that all the joy and delight that springs from the relationship will occur as magically as the doves which appear from nowhere out of a magician's hat. Hence not much skill and learning and insight and exertion will be necessary to maintain the relationship — or, if necessary, all learning and necessary knowledge and growth will come about spontaneously and harmoniously without too much struggle.

But there is also a magic in the instantaneous *recognition* of the uniqueness of the other person, and hence of our special bond. There is even magic in the *story* of the meeting, which seemed to be destined (*bashert* is the well-known word in the Yiddish language).

As usual, I suggest that the emotional tone of these magical connections has its roots in infancy. The magical sense of need-fulfilment and the magical recognition of uniqueness are so intricately related that I deal with them both concurrently.

The idea (from psychoanalysis) of "narcissistic omnipotence" suggests that the infant "thinks" that its needs are magically satisfied simply by having them. Simply feeling hunger, or pain, *makes* a "magical object" – mother – appear, who then magically feeds that hunger or heals that pain.

Surprisingly enough, it seems that psychoanalysis has been slow to apply the concept of "uniqueness" to the early infant. The processes generally described for early emotional development tend to be generalised for all infants and children (for example, Freud's stages from Oral to Anal to Genital) and any idea of an infant having a *unique sense of itself* is (to the best of my knowledge) not covered.

Of course, psychoanalysis might deal with the infant's sense of *specialness*, "thinking" it is the "princess" or "prince", or indeed, the "queen" or "king" — in short, thinking it has special entitlements, which really amounts to its narcissism. And psychoanalysis has specialist knowledge about how babies develop *a separate identity* from mother. This process is applied to all babies. But there is not much explicit reference to the baby's *sense of uniqueness*.

Let us examine this more closely.

It seems it is biology that has taught us about the uniqueness of new-borns for their mothers. To us humans, baby seals, penguins, turtles, and a host of other animals all look pretty much alike. Yet they are routinely recognized *as individuals* by their mothers, and they recognize her in turn, on the basis of the most one-dimensional, primitive, unique signals. It may be a unique smell, or a unique call of the young one to mother, or of the mother to the young one.

It works magically!

It is love at first smell!

Love at first sound!

In human infants there is now ample evidence of a parallel phenomenon: babies can recognize the unique smell or voice of mother. Even in the womb the foetus has been found to respond uniquely to mother's voice, or even to mother's dialect.

This is not learned behaviour. It is instinct. And what it amounts to is *a spontaneous bonding process — a perfect fit that happens magically.*

"Instinctually" here equates to "magically".

Instinct, effectively, *is* magic.

Instinct, effectively, is magic!

The bond is magical, and the bond is unique.

Mother and I don't have to *work* at attuning in with each other, don't have to negotiate or dialogue in any way as to what signals we shall designate for the sake of recognizing each other if there happen to be other infants and mothers around. And we certainly do not have to work at *desiring* each other!

It works magically! It is love at first smell! Love at first sound! We are "Soul Mates".   Now remember that this notion of "instant recognition", which amounts to "love at first sight" is precisely what was discussed as the first element of regression.

It is precisely this early-life magical perfect fit that we are trying to re-find, to re-create, in adult life when we are seeking the perfect Soul Mate. It involves love at first sight, a deep sense of uniqueness, and it happens, or is expected to happen, magically.

34

But this sense of uniqueness is primitive and simplistic — like the yin-yang sign, it is based on just a few simplistic, "one-dimensional" qualities in two beings which fit together perfectly. Later on, I shall discuss our developing complex uniqueness.

> "Love at first sight,
>
> and smell, and sound, and touch and feel"
>
> happens so uniquely and so magically.

However, one thing should be pointed out here: *there is nothing unique about uniqueness.* Every one of the baby seals or penguins is unique. Uniqueness is as common as pie. And this applies equally to simplistic uniqueness and to complex, developed uniqueness.

End of Magic of Special Uniqueness

NARCISSISM

You are my perfect need-fulfiller

Narcissism in the baby refers to how it knows (experiences) the mother *only* as a being that is there to fulfil its needs, and has not the slightest idea of her having a life, and needs, *outside* of her role as mother, and *outside* of her need to be there totally for her baby.

Narcissism in an adult in love reflects this. Of course, the adult now has enough consciousness and language to know that he is separate from the lover, and that this lover has needs outside of and unrelated to *his* needs. Yet he is incapable of seeing the *importance* of these needs to his partner, and he is not interested in exerting any energy to support his partner in fulfilling these needs in relation to the world outside of their relationship.

> The Soul Mate illusion contains the fantasy that all that I fulfil for you gives you all that you could possibly need — so that I am absolutely enough for you.

Not only is the infant unaware of his mother's separate needs, but he is also incapable of knowing that much of his own bliss and comforts come *from* mother, are his powerful response *to* mother, and are ultimately are caused *by* mother. *Sine qua non!* No mother, no bliss!

The infant has no sense of a separate identity from mother, or even of a boundary between them. So it only knows: "When things are good, they are good! What else is there?" There is a kind of non-verbal sense of "naturalness", a kind of "entitlement" to have its needs fulfilled. After all, "I am the being defined as 'he whose needs must be fulfilled'" (A popular expression I have heard from new parents about their baby is "He who must be obeyed.")

Such infantile "blindness" is appropriate to the life of the baby. But when I am an adult in an intimate adult relationship, and much of my personal strength and well-being is not inherently in *me*, but comes from the love and care my *partner* gives me, then I am narcissistic, and unaware of my narcissism.

I am unaware of the fact that I have re-created my blissful infantile state. I am unaware that my partner fulfils some of my unmet infantile and childhood needs, and heals my infantile wounds. I am happy here, fulfilled and strong, and healed, and that is all I am concerned about. Whether *she* is happy, and whether *she* has needs outside of this relationship, is not something I am particularly concerned about. Being regressed, my only concern is the fulfilment of my *own* needs. And I am stuck in an illusion of having solved life's essential problems around bonding.

> Thus, for instance, we might expect to be delighted in, given unconditional love, for being totally passive, for doing nothing, just for "being there", like a baby.

When we are not yet in a relationship, and still seeking our Soul Mate or romantic partner, the hope that we shall find a perfect need-fulfiller of the regressive kind is what constitutes narcissism in us. The perfect need-fulfiller will fill up the holes left by my mother's inadvertent inadequacies. And we may also be hoping for a perfect healer-partner — one whose love and care will understand and heal all the early-childhood wounds in me.

When we are actually in what seems to be a perfect-fit relationship (usually in the romantic phase), the feeling of being so "well-nourished" will hide any degree of our regressiveness. And we shall be under the illusion that we have solved all life's problems when it is really our partner who has given us the temporary solution to those problems.

If and when there is a breakdown in such a blissful seemingly perfect-fit relationship, narcissism consists in the belief and expectation that the partner should be the total fulfiller of our deepest regressive needs, and the perfect healer of our wounded infantile aspects.

For some men, forcing their partner to fulfil their needs is validated as a sign of their *masculinity*. In reality, it is a sign of their unacknowledged *vulnerability*. Often those have no sense of being inherently lovable try to get love by giving it, because they feel they have a right to demand that their partner fulfil their most important needs. (This "giving love to get love" is discussed in more depth later.) Such people are totally unconscious of their own self-centredness, and do not know how they are wiping out much of the reality of the partner they are connected with. Because such a narcissistic man, like a baby, is unconscious even of the *idea* of this extreme selfishness, he would never describe himself as "selfish" or "self-centred". In fact, he would consider that getting his needs fulfilled by others is a totally normal and healthy "masculine" way of being.

> For some men,
>
> forcing their partner to fulfil their needsis validated as a sign of their *masculinity*. In reality, it is a sign of their *vulnerability*.

I suggested above that the person in such a regressive, perfect-fit, "Soul Mate", "yin-yang" relationship has the feeling that she or he has thereby solved many of the essential life issues we all have to deal with. "Life issues" is a big subject, and we could fill an encyclopaedia with ideas about what these are or should be. In the field of psychology, the most popular writings about these suggest that different stages of life have different dominant issues or "crises" to deal with. The most well-known are Abraham Maslow's *Hierarchy of Needs* and Erik Erikson's eight (and later, nine) stages of social-emotional development. There is still debate about the nature of these. For instance, some believe that you cannot begin one stage unless the stage before it has been successfully completed. Others believe that *no stage is ever really fully completed*, and aspects of it are carried over into the next stage, where it may apply to new and different life skills and concerns appropriate to that age.

Naturally, these theories of the stages and ages of humanity suggest how we should normally grow, physically and psychologically from immaturity to maturity. They thus suggest to us some perspectives on what it means to be "adult". I just need to point out that for the purposes of this book, very little will be written about the nature of "adulthood" and all its complex parameters, especially in relation to love. What this book is pointing to are the life problems which have to be solved in the *earliest* years, the needs that are essential to be fulfilled, and how these very same problems and needs from this "stage one" can still be present in adult falling in love.

That is to say, *these needs of early childhood remain to be dealt with in all the later stages of life*. And since we are quite passive in the infantile years, these needs are mainly about *feelings, not actions,* and their validation or rejection by mother and father.

In adult life, the issues are similar, although they will apply to different life abilities, and hopefully have less intensity. Let me suggest some of what these might be. (Forgive the over-lapping.)

From the beginning of life and onward to death, we need to feel:

a. Basic trust —than we can rely on others to be care-full with us, physically and psychologically
b. Physical safety — being able to trust others not to be physically careless with us, not to expect us to be capable of doing more than we are capable of physically
c. Psychological safety — not to feel any sense of psychological cruelty towards us, like angry sounds, or looks of disgust
d. Safety from abandonment, that is, the feeling of being securely bonded
e. Delighted in, appreciated
f. Unique, different, *yet accepted* in one's group or society
g. Self-esteem, that one is a worthwhile, valuable member of one's group
h. A certain sense of respect for one's developing independence at an appropriate pace — hence not to have too intrusive a nurturance (usually called *engulfment*) nor too little nurturance and encouragement and support in our development (which is *abandonment*)

These life issues (or "problems to be solved") from "stage one" of life carry on their existence at every stage of growth of a human life, except that they apply to different functions, have application to the dominant activities and ways of being of any particular age. We need to be delighted in when we succeed in walking, and we get self-esteem from such delight in us. Later in childhood we might get self-esteem from being delighted in by having achieved a certain level of proficiency at ballet, or karate, or any other human skill requiring time and effort. Generally, we may say these life issues must be dealt with at any stage or age, in relation to the affairs, activities, feelings and so forth, of that age or stage. We do not expect a baby to do ballet. And we would not ordinarily praise an adult for the ability to walk.

As I said, I am only dealing with "stage one" (infantile) issues of life. The stage-and -age theorists suggest new and other issues arising later in life. But this book is not about those, because much has already been written about them.

When we have not outgrown our regressive infantile needs, and they get satisfied in an intimate relationship, so that suddenly we feel that all our life issues have magically been resolved, and our infantile and childhood wounds healed, we will feel deeply in love. We will feel that this person is the love of our life. *But this person is more likely to be one's re-created mother.*

We are thereby solving infantile states within us, not developed adult concerns. And our partner is the great solver of them. Thus, for instance, we might expect to be delighted in, given unconditional love, for being totally passive, for doing nothing, just for "being there" – just like a baby.

Narcissistic blindness, the lack of being able to see a partner clearly, consists of at least three things:

1. Not seeing that our "perfect-mother" partner has needs *outside* of fulfilling our needs — needs to be fulfilled by others in other ways, and needs to fulfil others in other ways.
2. Not seeing that no matter what we do, we *cannot* be a "perfect mother" for our partner, *cannot* fulfil all their needs and wants. Our partner needs fulfilment in areas and ways which we *cannot* give them, even if we wanted to.
3. Not seeing that because we might be perfectly nourished by a giving "perfect-mother" partner, our inner strength derives from *the partner's* presence, and that we have far less of such inner strength inherently inside us. We are being temporarily supported, given a crutch, not standing on our own legs. But we think we are!

WE ARE *ALL* NARCISSISTIC

Popularly we use the term "narcissist" above as if there really is such a defined person. We tend to divide the world into "narcissists" and "non-narcissists", as if there is a clear binary distinction, "us" and "them". So much of the time these days people are identifying *others* as "narcissists". I never hear of people referring to their *own*, inner narcissism!

But this itself is the most widespread narcissism in the world — the idea that narcissism belongs *to others* but *not to ourselves*. We *all* have areas of narcissism within us, which we need to recognize in order to grow as humans, and to become more effective as loving partners and compassionate human beings — because it involves recognizing and honouring the valid otherness of others. We all have blind spots to the reality of how life is in other people's skins, and most of us think that the inner experience of others is a carbon copy of our own. Hence we *think* we know what they need and are often incapable of listening to and/or tuning in to what they *really* need — very different from what we first imagined!

This author feels pretty sure that a certain very widely spread idea about loving one's self suggests a form of narcissism. There is so much written about how we must "learn to love ourselves — and not expect to get the love we need from others".

There is much wisdom in this . . . except . . . that perhaps it assumes that learning the loving of one's self takes precedence over learning the loving of *other* people! I am sure some thinkers might (validly perhaps) counter this with "well, you cannot love others if you cannot love yourself". (Interestingly enough, in the Gospel of Matthew we read:

And the second most important commandment is like this one. And it is,
"Love others as much as you love yourself".

(Matthew 33:29, Contemporary English Version.)

TWO FORMS OF NARCISSISM

I am going to describe here two possible forms of narcissism in actual intimate relationships — where the seeking and the hope and the expectations have in fact been actualised, and the perfect fit found:

1. In the first case, *you are my perfect mother* or parent, or, if you are not, I *expect* you to try and be so
2. In the second case, *I am your perfect mother* or parent, and when we have bliss, I fantasise that you are totally fulfilled by me; I *feel* that "I am enough for you, all you want and need as a lover" (even though *you* don't really feel that, but *I* refuse to see that).

When things are not perfect, I *expect* you to try to feel totally fulfilled by me.
Let us discuss each in turn.

1. YOU ARE MY PERFECT MOTHER

The first is when I relate from the child-in-me to my partner as the "mother" — I am projecting the image of the inner perfect mother I carry inside me onto my partner.

What happens here is that I, as "infant", have the fantasy that you are totally fulfilled by fulfilling my needs. I feel, especially in the early stages of a Soul Mate relationship, totally fulfilled by you, and in my imagination I see you as being totally fulfilled in yourself by your role of fulfilling me.

This is just as it was in the beginning, with me and mother, when I was suckling at her breast. I was not aware of her having a single need for herself *outside* of her need to see to it that all my needs were met; there was nothing she needed for *herself*.

Similarly, I have not the slightest idea that you have needs of your own *outside* of your extreme enjoyment of fulfilling *my* needs.

41

I feel, especially in the early stages of a Soul Mate relationship, totally fulfilled by you, and in my imagination, I see you as totally fulfilled in yourself

We see a parallel to this phenomenon in teenagers or young adults in relation to their parents. My parents are thought of as nurturers who simply have to be there for me, without needs of their own. They must not have doubts and uncertainties and ambivalences about their own relationship, not have needs outside of keeping the family together, safe and secure. Certainly, for most teenagers, it seems, their parents are not even supposed to have or need sex!

When, as a Soul Mate in love, I begin to start seeing cracks in my fantasy, when I see or feel you are not fulfilling all my needs properly, I feel anxious. And I might start *demanding* that you fulfil those needs, if you say you really love me. If you *don't* fulfil my needs, then you are a "bad" person, and this might hurt me deeply and make me sad. In response, I might get deeply angry and even aggressive.

I not only need, want, and desire that you fulfil my needs, but I *expect* you to fulfil them and I validate my expectation that you do so. That is, I give total credence to my expectation. I believe that you *should* fulfil my needs. And when you don't, I feel vulnerable and might even "throw my toys out of the cot".

I give very little validity or consideration to what my partner needs, because I am hooked on what I can get for myself out of this relationship. Now this might be "normal". But it is not healthy. (In *Falling for Love* I expand on this point that we tend to use the word "normal" to mean "healthy, good, etc." But at base, "normal" really just means "average", the statistical mean. As I pointed out, so much of human nature that is "normal" is actually very unhealthy, pathological, destructive, etc. To the extent that this is so, and in the multitude of areas where this is so, "normal" is *not* something to strive for.)

I have seen this phenomenon of romantic illusion both in my own youth, and in the lives of many others. Without exception, it goes like this:

When new love is blossoming, in all my dreams and visions my partner shares with me all the things of my life, and becomes part of my community.

My partner will come with me to all the sporting events I go to, will enjoy all my friends, will come to all my presentations at my local groups, will allow me to share with her/him my excitement about the stories I hear, or that play out in operas, or in the books I read, etc. etc. Most importantly, my partner will delight in all the sweet, cute things I do, all the unique eccentricities I am.

However, in my dreams and visions, do I do the same for my partner? On the contrary, I seldom imagine myself loving my partner's eccentricities. I seldom imagine that she/he dreams of how I will be a big part of her life, her friends, and her family. (In truth, her interests, her friends and her family will probably bore me to tears! And when that becomes evident, then my partner's fantasies about me being his/her perfect partner will be shattered.)

While writing, I have just remembered an even younger vision of how I believed love should look. I think I was in my mid-teens. My inner image of "The Girl", "The One", "The True Love" was of some delightful-looking creature in the *background* of my life, my hobbies, my interests, my homework, or whatever. And there she was doing absolutely nothing herself, *except* to delight in what *I* was doing. Her function was simply to give me total attention, love and appreciation for all the things in my life that *I* was engaged with — very similar, in fact, to when I was a child, with my mum in viewing distance, and ready to be asked for appreciation by me for any mediocre achievement of mine!

In other words, "The Girl" in that inner image was just like "Good Mum". She was merely an "appreciation machine", with no tasks of her *own*, and with no need to seek appreciation for herself. All she needed in order to make me love her was her extreme physical attractiveness and her deep appreciation for me. Apart from that, she had little purpose.

Hmmm. Would she have bored me as I grew to a wise young age! (Well, even when I was young, a few minor parts of me were indeed wise! As we all were!)

2. YOU ARE MY PERFECT NEEDY CHILD —Giving Love to Get Love

In Case 1 above I needed to get love by receiving love. In the present case, I need to get love, by giving love, and having it received by a needy partner. I become a perfect Soul Mate to you by ensuring that I supply you with all your needs. But I sacrifice my own needs.

From you, for this sacrifice, I expect to get love. I have the fantasy that I can detect all your needs, and that I am totally capable of satisfying them all, capable of satisfying them all totally. In return I expect the reward of getting some of my most desperate needs met. We are a perfect Soul Mate match, a beautiful yin-yang sign. Two beings perfectly enmeshed! This is often referred to as co-dependence.

Now co-dependence might work well as long as you remain regressed, a needy child needing nurturance. But once you start growing up and developing and becoming independent, you will discover that you have needs which I *cannot* in fact fulfil for you, needs which *others* can perhaps fulfil better.

But the Soul Mate illusion is about the fantasy that all that *I* fulfil for you gives you all that you could possibly need — so that *I* am absolutely enough for you.

However, *no person can be a hundred percent need-fulfiller for another.* The other person *always* has needs and desires that can only be fulfilled by someone *else*, and not the Soul Mate. (I am not suggesting these others must necessarily be sought out, but that at least that their reality be acknowledged.)

When all is bliss, I have the *fantasy* that you *are* totally fulfilled as a person by all that *I* give to you, that you need nothing more outside of what *I*, *uniquely* can offer you. I am everything to you; you need nothing and no one else!

When all is less than bliss, I have the *expectation* of you that you *should be* fulfilled by all I have to offer, and if I see signs that you are not, I start feeling vulnerable, anxious, with fears of being abandoned. I might start blaming you, or get angry, or even violent.

This narcissism often shows up in extreme forms in some adult humans, especially sociopathic males — who are totally and utterly blind that the other has needs separate from them, and who are stuck in the vision that anything and all that they do for their woman partner fulfils her.

An excellent if extreme case of this is that of Reg Kray, one of the famous Kray twins, criminals of London's East End during the 1950s and 1960s.

Reg Kray had no sense that his girlfriend had needs outside of his own. He imagined that everything *he* needed and wanted his girlfriend to be, *she* needed and wanted to be too —that by fulfilling *his* needs, she automatically fulfilled *her* needs.

And so it was he who decided how she would dress, what she would eat, and he provided all that for her. If she wished to go and choose her own clothes, he would hinder her, "lovingly" telling her that she no longer needed to do that, because he would do that all for her.

He seemed to be ignorant that his idea of what she needed might not concur with what she really needed to express her individuality. He totally blind-spotted any needs she might really have had, by pasting on to her a picture he thought was real and which, to him, showed exactly what she needed.

He had created a "perfect fit". He thought he was providing her with all she needed. He thought he was giving her "perfect love". Out of love for her, he even beat up men who seemed as if they had the slightest interest in her. "What a loving man, who shows his pure love by protecting his girl so!" He then even proved this by marrying her, out of pure love. But he was a giver of love who was deeply dependent on the receiver.

The image of a masturbatory fantasy lover comes to mind. Such a lover has no needs of her own, and "loves the way we make love with them". *We* have total control. *We* "move them around" in the picture in our head like a puppet on a string, so that they perfectly give us what *we* need to receive, or perfectly receive from us what *we* need to provide, in order to feel turned on. We don't really care if their needs are met or not, for they are just fantasies.

Reg Kray seems to have treated his girlfriend (and later wife) Frances in that way. He allowed her zero life of her own, and she, unfortunately, acquiesced. A year into their marriage, having been metaphorically "strangled", she took her own life.

Of course, in both cases above, the more ordinary of us might clearly be capable, as adults, of *seeing* the separate needs, the "different" areas of our partners which don't relate to us. But we *don't really ascribe much importance* to those, instead devoting our attention to seeking to get from our partner either directly, or indirectly, by giving to them.

Such blindness about mother is appropriate for a baby, but as adults romantically in love we are often stuck in this illusion — that the other automatically fulfils his/her needs by fulfilling mine. It mostly goes along with blindness about the fact that I do not have all of what my partner needs for her fulfilment.

And in the second case too, there is blindness to the fact that some of what my partner, this "child", needs is not something I am capable of fulfilling.

In summary, I see only those needs which you fulfil for me, and don't see, or give importance to, any needs you have for yourself outside of fulfilling my needs.

Where you *don't* fulfil my needs, I feel justified to *expect* you to try and fulfil those needs of mine. I have the fantasy that you are totally fulfilled in all your needs by what I give to you — because I refuse to see that you may have needs which I simply cannot fulfil, that you have needs outside of those which in fact I do fulfil for you.

If you are not fulfilled by all I give you, I *expect* that you should be so satisfied, and can get distressed or angry that you don't. That is, I validate and justify my right that "I am, or should be enough for you". But the reality is that I am not.

A (semi-)humorous quote I once saw on a postcard threatened: "If you do not let me make you happy, I will make your life a misery!"

Perhaps that quote captures the spirit of this in one sentence better than all my complex attempts. The point is that the giving is not genuine, caring, selfless giving. It is giving-to-get! It operates well in co-dependent relationships and is pure narcissism.

By contrast, true giving is giving-in-order-to-give — to see that the other gets what he/she needs *without* us needing anything from the transaction. And we *enjoy* being "givers".

In illusory Soul Mate romance, on the other hand, when we realize that our needs are not being fulfilled, and our justification about our expectation that they *be* fulfilled does not work – *that* is when our Soul Mate bubble finally bursts.

There is deep pain when a relationship breaks up.

One is no longer desired, no longer an object of one's partner's "possessiveness".

One is also no longer wanted for the emotional bond we created together for the two of us.

> The pain of breakup is understandable and acceptable. The anger and moral righteousness are understandable, but not acceptable.

NARCISSISM AND THE ART OF LETTING GO

The lessons from the breakup of relationships

There is deep pain when a relationship breaks up.

One is no longer desired, no longer an object of one's partner's "possessiveness". One is also no longer wanted for the emotional bond we created together for the two of us. Often this is accompanied by extreme moral judgments thrown at the "guilty" partner.

The pain is understandable and acceptable.

The anger and moral righteousness are understandable, but not acceptable.

They speak too loudly of infantile narcissism and possessiveness, of deep regressiveness. It is supreme proof of the implicit validation of the moral rightness of the narcissism and possessiveness during the happier phases of the relationship. It is a feeling of entitlement to be angry when my need to give, or my need to receive, are thwarted.

If one really loves the partner "just the way they are" there would remain some respect that comes from *philia*, the friendship element where we love the partner as a friend, outside of their ability to fulfil, or not, our most intense needs.

The high moralism when our partner leaves us, seemingly unfairly, is easy to see. It comes in forms like this:

"How could he/she?!"

"She should have realized that in a relationship you cannot . . . ! "

"Clearly, he should know . . . !"

"That's not the way things are done!"

"He was wrong to . . . !"

47

But that all this moralism is rooted in narcissism and regressiveness is not so clear to most of us.

That this is so is something we need to become aware of: "You have to protect me from my childish, vulnerable over-sensitivity, for I have not fully grown up yet. When you do not, you betray me and are bad and immoral".

The moralism starts even before the breakup. The partner who fulfils one's needs is deemed good; the partner who frustrates one's needs is deemed bad. It is a moral judgment based solely on one's own narcissism. It should go without saying that violence or cruelty towards such a partner cannot be justified by the rationalization that it is because one "loves" this person. Violence and cruelty are never love!

But the truth is that it is *nice* when one's needs are satisfied and one gets pleasure from them and our partner is *nice* for doing that, and it is *not-so-nice* when they don't do that. But that does not make them morally or ethically bad because they frustrate some of our neediness. "If you fulfil my needs, you are good; if not, you are bad!" — this surely cannot be a serious basis for a real moral and ethical evaluation of any human being. Yet this is what happens endlessly in all human societies.

> "If you fulfil my needs you are good;
> if not, you are bad".
> This surely cannot be a serious basis for a
> real moral and ethical evaluation of any
> human being.

End of Narcissism

DEPENDENCE

I am Small and you are Big

> On the day that you were born,
> the angels came together
> and decided to create
> a dream come true.

> – THE CARPENTERS

BABY/MOTHER BONDS VERSUS ADULT/ADULT BONDS

When discussing the fourth element of regression, Narcissism, I was asking you to consider whether you are managing to see beyond your own needs to get by receiving, and your own needs to get by giving, and to become aware of and accept the importance and significance of those of your partner's needs which you don't spontaneously see or spontaneously fulfil. You need to do that if you are to move from infantile love to a more developed real love, where you see your partner's *full* nature, including those areas where your needs are not necessarily related to each other.

In the present section I am asking you to consider whether you see your partner as much "bigger" than you. In that case, like mother to baby, your partner is seen as having amazing power to give you such a magical abundance of nurturance and support that your connection cannot be anything but the highest "beautiful blissful bond". (Naturally, when I talk of size, I am not talking of physical size but of ability, skill, power, or inner resources. Napoleon, for instance, though physically a small man, was militarily and politically a very "big" man indeed.)

In the affairs of the heart, size *does* matter!

It is crucial to become aware of this feeling that the provider of love is "bigger" than you, because it will help you to evaluate whether or not you are dependently regressed.

49

Consider this excerpt from a 1996 song sung by Celine Dion and others, "Falling into You", which seems to suggest the "bigger" lover, the "smaller" me. I would think that the person being sung to is seen as a very special "Soul Mate", but also as very "BIG"— certainly bigger than l'il ole me the singer! (I have paraphrased the words, because it costs a small fortune to get permission to quote even one line of the lyrics of a very popular song.)

You're a dream so true

I love falling into you

Love can't exist when we fear

To let each other into here

High walls begin to show a crack

And I begin to tumble down

Falling into you

I feel there is nothing that I lack

I'm like a leaf, like a star

Falling into who you are

Believing you'll never let me drop

Standing firm to catch me falling

Armed with strength that does not stop

(Songwriters of the original song: D'Ubaldo, Marie Claire / Nowels, Rick / Steinberg, Billy.)

Now the point is this: In order to let you "fall into me" I have to be big enough to contain you, big and strong enough not to "let you drop". In this connection, a small etymological digression might be enlightening.

The word "dependence" comes from the Latin *dependere*, which means "to hang from". Some baby animals hang onto their mothers, "depending" on them to be carried, and protected. And if you want to hang onto a branch of a tree, both the branch and the tree have to be strong enough to hold you. In short, the tree has to be "big".

There are a ton of song examples. They usually stress that my partner is my rock, my salvation. Or perhaps the "wind beneath my wings"(130) someone I simply cannot live without, cannot breath without, am nothing without. And so on.

In fact, this person might even be *named* "Mr Big": someone we desire more than anyone we know, someone who is perhaps not available – as for Carrie, in the TV series "Sex and the City". Note how "Mr Big" resembles mother, who, as we grow up, slowly begins making herself available *at her own convenience*, and, much of the time, expecting me to be alone and independent. "Mr Big" was that for Carrie.

The hundreds of songs which are hits clearly suggest that most folk see this "you are big, I am small" as quite normal. (But as I keep repeating: much that is "normal" is not necessarily healthy; in fact, is very often pathological). These lyrics arise spontaneously from the dreams and thoughts of songwriters and poets, and I see the population's total identification with the feelings expressed: "Yes, I would love to find such a big, all-giving lover!"

It must be understood, but not accepted as some sort of final solution to the search for love.

Note that society does not regard such songs as problematic or "sick" at all. We have to bless the writers for their creative expression of these deep soul forces in us. But we also have to see the regressive nature of these feelings, which need to be surpassed.

It is seen as the end of the search for love.

Such "Soul Mate love" is thus seen as wonderful, marvellous, the good, true and beautiful fulfilment of the very healthy search for love. It is seen as a great childlike state, sufficient unto itself, not in need of any development or surpassing. It is seen as the end of the search for love.

The "size difference" is not seen as a problem. If it is seen at all, it is regarded as a marvellous thing, because it simply means that I am getting all the more love by having found a rich source of love, a diamond mine, a treasure casket full of gold. In the affairs of the heart, size *does* matter!

Thus in dreams we might seek, and in romantic love appear to find, the bigger lover who brings us, on a powerful horse, much of what we need to feel fulfilled emotionally in life. No wonder the process of feeling blissfully bonded with someone is called "*falling* in love"!

In a nutshell, then, the common stance about all this is: "There is no problem". But I am suggesting that there *is* a problem!

The problem is that these kinds of relationships are a regression to a state where one partner is the "child" and the other is the "mother" – precisely the kind of relationship *beyond* which we should develop!

Our goal is not a child/mother relationship, but an adult/adult relationship.

What I am in fact suggesting is that romantic love, if it has this element of dependence, is something which must be surpassed, outgrown, not idealized or validated. It must be understood, but not accepted as some sort of final solution to the search for love. To rely on our partner to carry us, to rescue us, eternally, in our weak and vulnerable areas, and not to seek to grow out of such dependence and to develop ourselves via a process of becoming independent, means to remain infantile in some areas all of our lives.

— for the whole individual needs growing into, growing up to, and this has not happened yet.

It is probably worth noting, for the sake of clarity, that there are also dependencies of equals. That is, not all dependencies are of the big/small kind. There is a difference between a mother and child (big/small) dependency and that of two mature adults in a pair-bonded relationship (same-size).

If you need to play tennis, or dance, etc., you are dependent on a partner. But you and your partner are "same-sized". Of course you can dance alone, but you cannot have a two-person dance without a partner.

There is also a difference between *emotional* dependency and *factual* dependency. I am factually dependent on the bank. I need them; they don't need me. They are big; I am small. But I do not cry if we are "separated", and I can change banks with no feelings involved.

On the other hand, if I am emotionally dependent, I might feel sad if my tennis or dance partner breaks our appointment. I will be more than sad, perhaps rejected, if I *feel* that she is "big" and I am "small" — in which case my emotional dependence, hence my neediness, is bigger than a normal adult's. However, if we are emotionally adult and of "the same size", then I am mildly disappointed, but not devastated.

> **It is the *emotional* dependencies – when I feel "small", and you feel "big" – that speak of a state of regression.**

This is all to say that factual dependencies and emotional dependencies can both be of the big-small type or of the equal-size type. But it is the *emotional* dependencies – when I feel "small", and you feel "big" – that speak of a state of regression.

The movie, *Pretty Woman* is an archetypal Cinderella story

The distinction can clearly be seen in many of the blockbuster movies, like *Pretty Woman*, and the *Fifty Shades of Grey* series. In both cases the male is factually, powerfully, (and, in both cases, financially) very BIG. Something in those movies touched the heart, genitals, and hormones of absolutely millions of people.

Pretty Woman is an archetypal Cinderella story — a young woman of low status is "discovered", rescued from a difficult life, and brought into a higher status by a princely "Mr Big" who rides a big horse. At first she is dependent on him both factually (for money) and emotionally (for self-esteem and status and acceptance in society). Then, finding her feet, she becomes less of "just a prostitute, a beautiful body" and more "a person of unique value'. She begins to fulfil her potential, and her inner strengths and beauty show more and more. In short, she gets "bigger".

Later on in the book, in discussing the overcoming of dependency, I shall say more about this process. Here I simply want to illustrate the initial "size" disparity in Cinderella stories. It goes without saying that the woman will be emotionally vulnerable. But later in *Pretty Woman* some of the man's emotional vulnerability is shown too – although never to the point where he is *very* small or very vulnerable: he remains the big prince rescuing the small maiden). In fact, she has always had the dream of being rescued by a knight with sword on large horse. When, at the end, he does come to her, with flowers and "true love" but without ambivalence, the movie script explicitly describes him as carrying her to his (big) limo in such a way that her feet never touch the ground. Only "Mr. Big" can carry one so easily!

Note that at no point does she have any ambivalences about him. He is always the perfect man, with nothing she might see as a flaw. So the decision for them to be together is completely his.

The great success of this movie does, I think, point to how deep this need is in humanity — the need to be rescued by someone "bigger" than us. Of course, men have as deep a need to be rescued as women do. Yet, off the top of my head, I can't think of any blockbuster movies where a man is under the spell of a big woman, who rescues him, and in the end loves him un-ambivalently. (Who knows – perhaps my writings might inspire some producer or director to take the plunge!)

The *Fifty Shades* movie triptych also depicts the male as enormously big financially. But emotionally, he is more vulnerable than Richard Gere's character in *Pretty Woman*. In fact, Anastasia, the heroine in the *Fifty Shades* series, has an emotional hold over the hero — in the area of emotions and relationships, she is "big" to his "small". Eventually, at the end of the triptych, they have reconciled their private, secret, sado-masochistic fantasy sexual ways with the responsibilities of public life, adulthood, family, marriage, children, and work. And, of course, with adult and committed love.

TWO REASONS WHY ROMANTIC LOVERS FAIL TO NOTICE THEIR EXTREME DEPENDENCY

People in love seldom see their emotional regressive dependency very clearly, the "you are big, I am small". I think there are at least two reasons why this happens:

1.   THE DEPENDENCY IS MUTUAL

The first reason is that, more often than not, the dependency is mutual. Both partners have a small-to-big dependency on each other which makes the "transactions of love" *seem* like a mutual and beautiful interchange of equals. I suggest that this *seeming equality* hides the power that each has over the other; the regressive dependence that, in different areas of the relationship, each has on the other. Just as you are "big" to my "small" in some emotional and relationship areas, so too am I "big" to your "small" in my unique areas.

Thus a couple can both be "big" and "small", "mother" and "baby" to each other, *at the same time.* Each is a "child" to the other's "parent", and each is a "Goliath" to the other's "David". There might thus be an *illusion* of equality, a blind-spotting of this recognition of the other having enormous power as the "givers of love and delight" to us: "At last I am getting the love I have always sought!"

Because of the *mutuality* of power and neediness, there *seems to be* an adult equality. But this is an illusion.

2. THE SATISFACTION OF OUR NEEDS MAKES US FEEL STRONG AND INDEPENDENT

The second reason is that the satisfaction of needs makes us feel strong and independent —it makes it easy for us to validate such regressive dependencies as normal. When our stomachs are full we feel we can go without food forever. And when we feel that the source of nourishment is infinite, we feel nicely safe and secure.

But when we are hungry, our extreme dependence on food becomes clearly visible. And when the source of nourishment seems shaky and inconstant, we become vulnerable to potential loss.

> I feel this way, not because of what you have done to me.
> I feel this way because of who I am.
> I am the cause of my feelings, because it is I who respond in this way to this kind of behavior in you, because of who I am.

Mother has incredible power over the child, to satisfy its extreme neediness, or frustrate it.

When the infant is frustrated, it tends to "throw its toys out of the cot". Of course, when these needs are totally fulfilled, then the world seems "right", and, for a while, the extreme underlying neediness is masked. The baby has no distress, feels fine, satisfied, omnipotent.

And so it is with "True Love".

When "True Love" has been found and a regressive beautiful *blissful* bond has been created (re-creating one's mother-infant bond), it *seems* as if it is the forever answer to all the problems of life. When long-held needs are at last fulfilled, the *feeling* of neediness and dependence disappears.

55

The same applies if a beautiful *healing* bond has been created. The satisfaction of extreme neediness masks the extreme neediness lying just beneath the surface. Like health that is taken for granted when we have it, we find no reason to question it or attend to it. But when it leaves us, our previous vulnerability to sickness is suddenly exposed.

Let me point out here, however, that the extreme neediness and excitement stimulated by the promise of love is *normal*, and not at all an unusual state applying only to those who had a problematic childhood. The attempt to re-create the infantile bond is, I believe, in all of us. But with greater experience of feeling love and delight for potential partners in our youngest, "courting" years, some of us manage to have insight into infantile love, and grow beyond it.

Nevertheless, those who have had difficult or inadequate early years are likely to feel far more insecure and on shaky ground as adults in love than those who have had "good-enough mothering" (in the words of Donald Winnicott, a major psychoanalyst in this field). However, *nothing that happens to us in childhood necessarily excludes us from the possibility of finding love and giving love.*

So, this emotional dependence we have on the other becomes invisible *until* love is withdrawn, seemingly or actually. Suddenly we are hurt, angry, betrayed, feeling almost as distressed as babies. Conflict ensues. Wounds are re-opened. Our small/big dependence becomes visible.

If the other no longer loves us, either we feel totally unlovable and lose our self-esteem, or we get angry with and judge the withdrawer of love as bad or even positively evil. But they are neither of these. The feelings and responses for which we blame our partner are *actually due to who we are ourselves.*

I do not feel this way because of what you have done to me.

I feel this way because of who I am.

I am the cause of my feelings, because it is I who respond in this way to this kind of behaviour in you, because of who I am.

If I lose my self-esteem because you have rejected me, that loss is due to my own lack of inherent self-esteem, and not because you have *robbed* me of my self-esteem. (I analyse this in more depth when discussing Marshall Rosenberg's work in my book *Falling for Love.*)

So, in the breakdown of the strong beautiful blissful bond, the degree of our dependence and regressiveness is revealed, as is the "largeness" of our partner (the power he or she holds over us, the extreme neediness we feel towards them).

Of course we may feel the pain of separation, but that does not have to go with any loss of self-esteem.

For people who are very emotionally regressed, most of their factual dependencies will have a strong and passionate emotional component. Fulfilled, they will feel *enormously* so. Frustrated and unappreciated, they will feel abandoned, forlorn, unattached, distressed — and small. They will have trouble feeling secure in the sense of belonging, a solid sense of being part of "us" — they will feel like outsiders. When rejected, they feel small and vulnerable, both factually, and emotionally. For them the whole world is "mother's breast" – which is either satisfying them or frustrating them; keeping them bonded, attached, "in the loop", or casting them out in the desert, deserting them.

The beatific and successful public image of such types comes more from the public love and appreciation they get than from themselves. Without that public love and appreciation, they feel valueless. But while we see them being so enormously charming, successful, apparently confident, we might not know it is on the shakiest of grounds. They do not feel *inherently* confident and successful. They need *public* acclaim and love. Often, unexpectedly, such celebrities commit suicide — especially when their public acclaim ends. Or sometimes even in spite of that acclaim.

To put all of this in other words: when I see you as figuratively very big and me as figuratively very small, I am reliving the memory of my early child/mother bond, where I was literally small, and she was literally big. When I want to be delighted in by someone "big" and special like you, and am not seen as interesting at all, I am very distressed. The attachment I am trying to create, the delight in me I am trying to get from you, my trying to make you and me into "us", is failing. (132)

Many of our needs for love should ideally be satisfied in infancy, childhood and youth, and surpassed to some extent. So having extreme neediness for these things *as adults* is a sign of our regressiveness. Those needs and processes should already have been surpassed and outgrown.

However, it is unrealistic to expect most of us to have had such a perfect, unwounded upbringing. So, on the one hand, we need to have compassion for each other's wounds. On the other hand, we are simply wrong in expecting our intimate relationships to be the great fulfiller of these desperate childhood needs, and, thereby, to be the great healer of such wounds. This expectation, this belief that our partner should be our great healer by being the great satisfier of unmet childhood needs, is often the cause of conflict in intimate relationships.

By the same token, the less regressed we are, the more solid we are in our own self-love, the less wounded we feel when rejected, the less we "take it personally". Of course we may feel the pain of separation, but that does not have to go with any loss of self-esteem.

JEALOUSY — A LESSON IN SIZE

There is one phenomenon which most of us have experienced which easily helps us understand emotional "size". When we feel jealous about our partner's attachment, or seeming attachment to someone else, we experience the emotional size of that rival as "big", perhaps even as "enormous", and certainly as threatening, creating fear of abandonment in us.

Often that person, before becoming or being seen as a rival of some kind, is experienced as an equal, or even as smaller than us, not very interesting, boring, hence lacking power and ability to take our partner away from us. But as soon as we see that our partner is deeply interested in that person, sees great value in them that we do not see at all, then suddenly that same person is seen as a rival, and their metaphorical size increases enormously. Being "bigger" than us, they are a threat to us.

In infancy and early childhood, we experience the enormous power of Father, for whom Mother leaves us to cope alone. With his Oedipus Complex hypothesis, Sigmund Freud suggested that the young boy has fantasies of getting rid of the father, in order to have the pleasure and nurturance and bliss of mother all for himself. Such "largeness of size" of our "rival" is re-created, re-presented, in adult eternal triangle situations. (133)

I recently had occasion to post a Facebook comment about a photo of Hugh Hefner, the Playboy magazine magnate, sitting, in his old age, amid about 150 shapely Playboy "bunnies". My comment went something like this: Hefner has successfully eliminated all male rivals, managed to take the most nubile females of the pack for himself, thus declaring himself the most dominant ape, the "largest" in size.

I don't know to what extent he saw those females as full humans in their own right. My psychoanalytic thinking would incline me to see all those warm bodies as representative of "mother's body" — warm physical nourishment that Hefner would have all for himself. In other words: "I, Oedipus, have defeated my rivals (Symbolic "Father" and all other men), and have succeeded in having 'mum' all to myself"!

THE WORLD'S GREAT PASSIONATE LOVE AFFAIRS

There has been a tendency in world literature to regard the great and famous passionate love affairs as examples of extraordinary true love. This thinking is a defence of great passion where two people are satisfying (and sometimes frustrating) mutual small-big relationships with each other. I would argue that many of them are examples of extraordinary regressiveness masquerading as great love. Each partner is validating the childish regressiveness of each other, rescuing the other from her or his childhood wounds, yet making sure the other remains dependent, because that would "prove" that the love is "true".

But it's all a grand illusion. The mutuality of the neediness also conspires to hide it.

The deep, intoxicating experience of powerful needs fulfilled might certainly *look*, to our culture's normal myopia, like amazingly passionate and thus "obviously" real love. But underlying the intensity of passion where, temporarily, needs are totally satisfied, is great desperation, and great neediness.

Only when, as inevitably happens, something tears these powerful bonds apart at the seams, is the extreme desperation of the neediness revealed. Often great drama, betrayal, or even murder is played out. That is to say, powerful regressiveness is revealed.

A perfect example of that is the extreme passion of two famous actors, Richard Burton and the very beautiful Elizabeth Taylor. They married and divorced each other twice. She had fallen for love and married eight times, and he, five. They were both alcoholics — a clear state of regression. Unable to cope with real life, they chose fantasy life — *imagining* that they could satisfy the deep regressive needs for love in each other.

I suggest that each was extremely "big" for the other's "small". According to Wikipedia:

Burton said that he turned to the bottle for solace

"to burn up the flatness, the stale, empty, dull deadness

that one feels when one goes offstage." (155)

SOUL-MATE-SEEKERS SEEKING LOVE

When, on dating websites, Soul-Mate-Seekers post what they are seeking, it seems to suggest both the narcissistic passivity of the Fourth Element of Regression, plus this emotional dependence, the "I am small, you are big", of this Fifth Element. Incurable romantics usually have less thought-out ideas than Soul-Mate-Seekers about love. So when *they* post, the same elements are there – for example, the prince on the powerful white horse who will come and carry the passive maiden away. She only thinks of narcissistically getting *her* needs met. And she thinks of herself as "small", while her shining knight is "big".

Horse and Prince are big! Heady and strong! Princess is small!

All she has to do is hang around and wait. She must keep her hair washed and brushed, and wear nice seductive clothing.

On the contrary, the Princess waiting for the knight in shining armour on the white horse should acquire a horse of her own, and learn to ride it! One day the two will ride together, but each on a horse of their own!

Indeed, it is not only females but also males who are waiting for the "knight-ess" in shining armour who will come on a white horse to carry *them* away. All I need do is "suck" on the "milk of human kindness" of that great "nurturing breast" and drink from that fountain of nourishment and strength. Then she will make me feel better, and I will grow spontaneously.

Just as I did with mother!

the Princess waiting for the knight in shining armor on the white horse should acquire a horse of her own, and learn to ride it! One day the two will ride together, but each on a horse of their own!

End of Dependence

A SENSE OF BOUNDARYLESSNESS
"We are One"

Accompanying dependence and narcissism in romantic lovers is a sense of no boundary between thee and me. I don't know where I end and you begin, where you begin and I end. We are one. We are merged, in bliss.

Similarly, for the early infant, there is no sense of a boundary separating it and mother, and it and the world. Rather, for the baby, mother *is* the whole world.

This begins right in the womb. In the womb we experience a floating, "oceanic" boundaryless state in which there is no difference between our insides and our outsides.

Once we are born and (hopefully) start breast-feeding, we experience a similar bond with mother. For the early infant, there is no sense of "me and mother". Like Soul Mates, we simply are "One". It does not even make sense to describe us as "Us" — there is no "Us". Everything that is in my whole young world is simply one quagmire of sensations. I experience no boundary between myself and mother. There is only "One". (101)

Of course, when the infant feels good, the real reason is that it has been well nurtured all round. But it is possible for the infant to have painful, inner, "growth pains" not caused by a lack of nurturing. Whether the infant's pain or pleasure is generated from itself or from mother, it is all experienced as "one". So when "I" feel displeasure, for whatever cause, (my self, or mother), it is both myself and "the world" which is in a bad, dis-pleasurable state. For me, there is no world that exists outside of my inner state (which is projected outside of my skin to "the world", which is basically mother) and no inner state that does not speak of the state of "the world".

When there is happiness, there is happiness all round. When there is pain, all the world, me, and mother are in pain, though the infant does not distinguish between the three things. Because of this, there is no identifying of what causes what — or I should say of who is doing what to whom.

Psychoanalysis talks of the baby's omnipotent fantasies —that it "thinks" it causes its needs to be met *simply by having them*. It is probably frustration of need which teaches the baby that there is a distinction between it and mother, and that its good feelings, as well as its bad feelings, are caused mainly by what mother does for it.

So then, frustration "teaches" the infant its boundaries, its separation from mother. Frustrated, the infant has to figure out who is doing what to whom — finally realizing that it is mum doing this to me. But before this realisation, there is not much sense of who is doing what to whom, because there really is no "who" and no "whom".

The main point to be made here is that sometimes Soul Mates and romantic lovers also speak of this "I don't know where he ends and I begin". They speak of being "merged" and they speak of not knowing quite who is doing what to whom, that is, they cannot locate cause and effect for the incredible bliss they feel as bliss bunnies.

But there is an element of regression operating here. I suggested that we should become aware of such powerful regressions in what appear to be "positive" relationships, such as Soul-mate-seekers and romantics seek and temporarily find. The narcissism I described suggested that we think that the *other's* needs are fulfilled automatically by their fulfilling *our* needs. Also, the emotional dependence that seemingly operates so satisfactorily, so nourishingly, helps with this sense of no-boundaries. This is part of the process of feeling as "One" — the perfect flow between needs needed and needs fulfilled helps create the illusion of boundarylessness.

In Soul Mate relationships this is a two-way process. It all seems very happy. We are "One" and I don't know where you begin and I end, where I begin and you end. That is, I do not know where the boundaries between us are, and, who cares, we don't need those boundaries anyway. As with our good mums, in the womb and at their breasts, we have found and created a good thing here. We feel omnipotent. Just by being who we are, our needs are met. Let us not rock the boat.

As long as they are blissfully connected, Soul-mate-seekers and Romantic Lovers are unconcerned about who is doing what to whom. It's all magic, boundless and boundaryless. But when things go awry in the relationship, suddenly they begin to allocate blame about "who is doing what to whom".

Normally, it is the *other* who is blamed. But normal, as I keep reiterating, is often not the healthiest way of functioning. More enlightened couples are more likely to try to solve their relationship problems *without* blame, and *with* love and compassion. That is to say, "am *I* responsible for this, or are *you*?" (This is discussed in much depth in *Falling for Love*).

Earlier on, I gave the example of the English criminal Reg Kray. He could not conceive of a boundary between him and his girlfriend, who eventually took her own life.
A similar extreme example concerns another deeply pathological habitual criminal. His comments in an interview suggest a baby's fantasy of complete control of the mother's breast being symbolized in adult behaviour (137):

There is a rush knowing that you are one-step ahead.

We do the crimes in luxury vehicles. You feel like a semi-

god... You walk into a house knowing you can take

what you like. There is nothing that is not yours.

I knew right from wrong, but did not give a damn!

That is to say, his adult social brain part knew how his actions would be seen by society, but in his regressed, fantasy world, "mother's breast" (read: "the whole world") belonged to him, and he could take it whenever he wanted to. What he needed, he would have! His bond with "mother" was perfect. The sense of omnipotence created by his criminal activities dissolved any boundaries coming between his needs and the suppliers of their fulfilment. (Most probably, he was seriously deprived in the womb and in infancy. And now, in adult life, he was trying to compensate.)

There are some destructive adult relationships which are so regressed that the couple truly regard themselves as one. (In some cases, it only applies to one of the couple.)   Such relationships are generally called "co-dependent" and are formed by two people who have both had serious childhood bonding problems. A prime example in literature of such a couple is brilliantly expressed in Edward Albee's 1962 play *Who's Afraid of Virginia Wolf?* This was also made into a movie with famous real-life co-dependent "Soul Mate" couple Richard Burton and Elizabeth Taylor. She was married eight times, and twice to Burton. Later in life, he realised that they each had serious regressive problems needing to be looked at.

But these two examples are of powerful, famous, regressed destructive relationships. I suggest too that we should be aware of such powerful regressiveness in what appear to be very average "positive" relationships, such as Soul-Mate-Seekers and romantics seek and temporarily find.

End of Boundarylessness

AMBIVALENCE OVERCOME

"Love has overcome Mixed Feelings"

In infancy, we learn that mother seemingly has both a good side (when she nurtures us blissfully) and a bad side (when she frustrates us temporarily). We thus develop "mixed feelings" towards her — or what is referred to as "ambivalence".

Naturally we want to experience more of the pleasure, and less of the pain. To put that differently, we wish to overcome the ambivalence, and stay within, or return forever, to the beautiful blissful bond state. If the infant had language and could think things out, it would presumably not yet, at this tender age, decide that "I will take the good with the bad". Rather, it would want to go back to the good, forever.

I suggest that this path, backwards rather than forwards, is what happens when we romantically expect love to be blissful forever. It is why some Soul-Mate-Seekers and incurable romantics pull out of relationships when they are not perfectly blissful.

> We are in the Soul Mate illusion — the incurable romantic illusion that ambivalence has at last been overcome, now and forever more, amen!

As teenagers and young adults in the Western world, we experience lots of different relationships. We fall so in love (sorry, *for* love) with someone. Well, older and wiser people call it "infatuation"— which the *Aa dictionary* on my Apple computer defines as "a short-lived very intense passion for someone". Because of their rejection of us, or mixed feelings about us, the desired love affair does not happen and we have to move on.

Mostly we to go through a variety of love objects where *we have mixed feelings about them* — each has strengths and weaknesses, as we see these. And so we eternally have mixed feelings, until … well, one day, "true love" comes along, and we meet someone about whom we no longer have mixed feelings. We are "in love". Love has spontaneously happened, and there are no skills to learn about how to be a loving partner or person.

We are in the grip of the Soul Mate illusion — the incurable romantic illusion that ambivalence has at last been overcome, now and forever more, amen!

The tremendous excitement surrounding highly romantic engagements and marriages speaks volumes for the recreation of this childhood joy. In this, the "good" side of the simple ambivalent world, things seemed to happen more magically than in the complicated ambivalent world. So we reach back for this "childhood innocence", where the world is a magical place and rabbits and doves spontaneously come out of hats, and conflicts spontaneously disappear (like the lady in the box), without the need for effort, struggle and complex decision-making. Conflict gets resolved magically too (the woman sawn in half is magically restored).

This is easier, less stressful, and avoids conflict. But it also wipes out the richness of the real complexity of our lives. Because in the difficult ambivalent world, we are more aware of causality, of what *really* causes what. And this removes the childish magic of the world, the sense of things happening mysteriously and wondrously. We know "how the magician performs the trick" and this makes the whole show "boring". But it is "boring" if all we are seeking in relationships is "magic". And especially if we are incapable of *making* magic and gleaning joy from the *ordinary*. (In what follows, I will have more to say about this "overcoming of ambivalence".)

Note that in Soul Mate relationships, the ambivalence is "overcome" by regression, not progression. It has been "overcome" by going backwards, by eliminating the bad, the frustrating, and indulging in the good, the pleasurable and comforting.

The famous psychoanalyst Melanie Klein taught us that early infants see mother either as *totally* good, *totally* fulfilling, and pleasurable, or as *totally* bad, frustrating, pain-and causing. Initially, they are unable to put the two states together as referring to the same person, mother.

Remember that the infant is living out of time. Feeling happiness means feeling it *forever* — "living happily ever after", in the phrase of the fairy tales. And similarly, feeling pain means feeling that *forever* — condemned to hell for eternity, in the phrase of religious texts.

The point about these two states characteristic of early infancy is that they are binary — they are either/or. Either the mother is *totally* good, pleasurable, nourishing, or she is *totally* bad, pain-causing, frustrating. In both cases these are strong reactions to powerful stimuli.

Later, says Klein, the infant "attains ambivalence" and can see that the two states can be caused *by the same person*. The two states can move from being either/or to being both/and: my mum is both good *and* bad, frustrating, *and* pleasurable — each in its own time and each totally and purely so! About this there is little the infant can do but accept it.

So, in adult romance too, ambivalence *will* return!

In fact, psychologists generally consider that *all* human relationships contain ambivalence. In other words, we are condemned, or indeed blessed, to have mixed feelings toward *everyone* we meet, not just our loving partners.

We know "how the magician performs the trick" and this makes the whole show "boring". But it is "boring" if all we are seeking in relationships is "magic". And especially if we are incapable of *making magic*

and gleaning joy from the *ordinary.*

If we consider cases of romantic love where the bubble bursts, it means that the relationship goes through a stage of *total* bliss and then a stage of *total* pain, dissatisfaction, alienation and so on. Naturally, as adults, we know that these relate to the same person. So now, seeing that we have seen "two sides" of a person, and realize the "good", bliss-producing side is not the *only* side they have, and not the *only* side that we see, we have to make a decision as to how we will proceed.

But we know we are dealing with a both/and situation. As adults, we have the ability to choose, and can decide. (My suggestion as to how we could and should go forward with this comes in the next section.)

Of course, it might be that it is not the "bad" side *of the partner* that has raised its dissatisfying head. It might be *in ourselves* that we discover a flipside which originally thought that this partner was perfectly what we wanted. But now we are not so sure.

Whether the ambivalence arose from the partner, or from ourselves, incurable romantics and Soul-Mate-Seekers might find themselves really disappointed, and wish they could re-find or re-create that previous pure bliss. People who are more "realistic" might decide to "take the good with the bad", to try and cope with and find a way to tolerate the bad, for the sake of having the pleasurable sides of the partner. That is, they tolerate the ambivalence. They realise that this is what we all need to deal with in intimate relationships.

And for some of us, when the hope of "true love" is dashed, the result might be a feeling of eternal hopelessness about *ever* finding love. But only if we are stuck at this level of ambivalence, and believe it was indeed "true love" that was lost.

BIPOLAR— THE ILLUSION OF BLISS

An extreme example of this escape from the difficult ambivalent world, an escape all the way back to *pre*-ambivalence, occurs in the lives of people suffering from bipolar disorders. Here we have an extreme example of just how illusory bliss can be.

When bipolar people, going off their medication, enter a manic phase, they are so positive, so delightful, so energetic, so happy, that they fool many people with their extreme positivity. Perhaps we should call this manic phase the "magic phase". Manic bipolar people often inspire people, make big money deals, sign huge contracts, and so on. But it is all based on illusion, unreality, it is all a projection of "good mother" (or "good breast") onto the world, recreating the positive side of that early childhood *pre*-ambivalent state.

However, remember that the infant, when in *one* state, is totally unable to remember the *other* state, the flip side of the reality of the connection to the love object – with resulting disconnection, severe depression, guilt, and so on. "Mother" is projected onto the world, which is either *totally* good, magical, joyful and all-nourishing, or *totally* bad, shaming, depriving, punishing, frustrating, and empty. So these bipolar people fall into long depressions — once more *totally* misperceiving the real nature of the world and its people.   Each   state sees the world from the point of view of its own projections, and each state has little relationship to the world and others as they really are. Bipolar people have not yet, in Melanie Klein's phrase, "attained ambivalence", have not yet been able to integrate the world (which in their case is mainly a mother projection) into both good *and* bad. The "mixed feelings" of the world, hard enough for most of us to deal with, are far from integrated in persons going through bipolar episodes.

End of Ambivalence overcome

67

OVERCOMING

THE

ELEMENTS

OF

REGRESSION

OVERCOMING THE ELEMENTS OF REGRESSION

Real love means mature love, which means that our regressive natures have to be dealt with, and eventually surpassed. The bliss of romantic love is so often based mainly on these areas of regression, which, in their magical pleasure, hide their basic immaturity.

This is not to imply that mature, grownup love means boring love. It means finding *adult* forms of excitement. It also allows childlike joy ample space and time for playfulness, childlike innocence and basic trust. But not to the extent that those take precedence over adult functioning, adult goals, adult tasks, and adult pleasures.

As individuals, and as a species, we are still immature in our ability to love. One just has to look at the magnitude and scope of lovelessness in the world, both in intimate relationships, and in relationships generally. We see an endless array of couples struggling to love creatively, or behaving destructively toward each other. As individual lovers, and as a species, we have to grow up,

In this section I offer suggestions about what such growing up entails, in relation to each of the *Elements of Regression* I have discussed. Being aware of these elements, we might perhaps be better informed as to which roads we need to travel so as to become better at the art of loving.

Here is a timely reminder of the seven elements of regression which glue romantic couples together:

THE SEVEN ELEMENTS OF REGRESSION

1. Narcissism (both in Giving and Getting)
2. Dependence
3. No Boundaries
4. Ambivalence
5. Magical Processes (Narcissistic Omnipotence)
6. Recognition of (special, rather than ordinary) Uniqueness
7. Love At First Sight

CONFLICT RISING

One of the main spoilers, when romantic love starts falling apart, comes from conflict. Whereas *in the beginning* we found endless differences in each other which delighted us, *now* we begin to find differences which don't delight. (In *Falling for Love,* I wrote copiously of how conflict, used creatively, can be a great opportunity for increasing intimacy in a relationship.) We certainly get to know each other at a deeper level, and if we can come through conflict well, we become more intimate, and really intimate, at that – intimate with the *truth* and the *reality* of each other.

In *Falling For Love* I also suggested that what sustains and fuels conflict is judgmentalism, the very easy putting down of each other, "disssing" each other, calling each other "wrong". I suggested that it was vital we see how our own judgmentalism fuels the conflict with our partners, and how, in order to be true lovers, we need to examine our own judgmentalism. In fact, in *Falling For Love*, I wrote copiously about the nature of judgmentalism.

But what also fuels conflict is an *expectation* that the regressive elements should yield beautiful blissful bonding. And when the bliss has disappeared, the *partner* is blamed.

<u>Come with me now as I go through the seven elements and sketch out how conflict might be generated by these unrealistic, dysfunctional expectations.</u>

If I expect my partner to be *totally fulfilled by fulfilling me*, and she is not, I may get angry and frustrated. If I fail to see that she has needs outside of her needs which are fulfilled by the relationship with me, my partner might (justifiably in this case) be angry and frustrated with me. My *narcissism* sustains the conflict.

If I expect my partner to be *so much bigger than me*, and to be able to hold me when I am at my smallest, and my partner simply is not that "big", I might judge her to be inadequate, and conflict is likely to ensue from such *dependence*.

If I was so happy that we had *no boundaries* between us, and my partner, for healthy and growthful reasons, decides that for our mutual growing up, some boundaries must be set, and I feel betrayed by this "breaking of a sacred bond", conflict is likely to ensue.

If I expect my partner to feel totally *un-ambivalent* towards me, and she is not, I might, childishly, feel unloved, abandoned and even cheated by my partner, and this can cause conflict. I might be a totally irresponsible child, but for this I expect unconditional love!

If my partner no longer seems to be *magical* to me, or fails to regard *me* as magical, and I blame her for that, this will "magically" fuel conflict.

If my partner no longer sees me as *specially unique*, but as "you are the same as *other* men/women! I thought you were *different*", and I expect her to love me as special and unique, I might blame her for not seeing me that way. And this should go a good way to providing a reason for conflict. In this case my

70

partner no longer sees me as that special simplistic unique being that she or he saw when we first fell *for* love at first sight.

In the next sections, I will suggest some directions we have to go if we are to give up our regressiveness and its limitations, and if we are to grow up and really love another different, separate person.

1. NARCISSISM

— THE CENTRAL ELEMENT OF REGRESSION TO BE OVERCOME

Overcoming our narcissism entails, first, recognising that we have added things onto our vision of our new partner that were not really there, and, second, withdrawing those projections. By this process, we begin to see our partner, and our mutual situation, more clearly. It includes withdrawing the *expectation* that our partner should be re-creating that feeling of our early infantile love of all our needs being perfectly met. If one is not in an intimate relationship, and hoping for one, it involves trying to be aware of some of the unrealistic expectations we may be harbouring in our seeking for a partner.

So, in summary, it involves recognising withdrawing the projections and the expectations that:

1. Our partner will create nothing but perfect bliss, fulfil all our needs, and that conflict (separation) will be overcome spontaneously, all with the greatest of ease, so that there will be no skills to learn about how to be a loving partner.
2. Our partner will fill all the holes left in us from a partially inadequate childhood (which we have *all* had) and be the magician who makes us feel whole again.
3. Our partner will heal all our childhood wounds, so that we can at last put our painful pasts *in* the past, and get on with our lives.

It is a realisation that the *Soul Mate bliss* of a perfect bond is a *regressed bliss*. A blissful bond that mimics the infantile perfect bliss of a baby (or foetus) attached to its mother when it needs are perfectly fulfilled — when there is no real sense of a psychological separation of the infant from its mother.

Overcoming our narcissism therefore includes the realisation that our partner *cannot* fulfil *all* our needs, and *is not deficient or "bad" because of that*. It involves too the realisation that they have needs for their own fulfilment that are unrelated to us in any way — that they need things for *themselves* which *we* cannot give them, and that they do in fact have other needs *outside* of any need they have just to satisfy *our* needs.

What this comes down to is that our partners have needs they need to fulfil outside of an intimate relationship — needs both to get, and to give, in *other* relationships. Most of these, of course, are adult needs, needs for adult company different to their partner, or to play sport, or have hobbies, or entertain themselves, or indulge in any variety of activities which they cannot do with their partner. At the most basic level, mature love means being able to *support* one's partner in fulfilling these needs unrelated to us out of our love for them as *separate beings*.

But it is precisely the partner's sense of bonding with others outside of an intimate relationship which might be the most threatening to one's narcissism. The sense that our partner is not only enjoying an activity *outside* of our relationship, but feels a strong bonded connection to that person or activity is something that may threaten a narcissistic lover.   *However, if you want to be a real true lover to your partner, you will have to love and support your partner's bonding with those others, or those other activities.* Jealousy, insecurity, feeling threatened, especially when there is actually no threat from our partner, are *the surest signs of our regressiveness, of not having overcome our narcissism.* To really love your partner means to have joy, delight, and acceptance of their close bonds to the other. Unable to do that, we are not able to love maturely.

And, for every one of us, there is always the potential of *other* deeply intimate relationships, different to, but equally possible to our current most beloved partner.

The same applies for our partner.

We can measure our own narcissism and regressiveness by the over-reactive pain we feel when rejected by someone whom we feel could satisfy certain emotional needs of ours; but also by the over-reactive joy we feel when someone *does* in fact satisfy some desperate regressive need of ours, such as those I suggested that solve "life problems".

When we feel this, it is time to look at ourselves, to seek help or perhaps even therapy. If instead, we feel *entitled* to blame our partner for our state of pain, neediness and desperation, then we are out of love completely, and have created, both for ourselves and for our partner, a situation of lovelessness.

> **When the need for appreciation, to be delighted in for our achievements, is as intense in adulthood as in childhood for our passivity, we are certainly in a regressed state.**

BEING ADULT LOVING RATHER THAN REGRESSIVELY NEED-FULFILLING

What does it mean to be fully adult rather than a regressed child or infant even when one is already grown up? Well, we all have some ideas about this, and are ready to call someone "childish" or regressed when they behave in a certain way we consider to be "non-adult". This author has racked his brains about this differentiation and realised that here we are dealing with a quagmire. The reason is that many things that develop in infancy and childhood must healthily be carried through to adulthood. Equally, many things have to be left behind. This means that adult life is a multi-coloured, multi-layered quilt containing parts of many ages all woven together into a complex pattern. (Psychologists have attempted to map out the stages or ages of life. The most popularly known of these attempts is that of Erik Erikson.)

It seems clear and easy to say that no adults should seriously think they are capable of real love if their love is of the nature of the "elements of regression", which relate to the first two years of life. But then how shall we describe a more mature, adult kind of love?

If we are going to describe this in terms of needs, one point is that adult needs are clearly different from infantile needs. They are different in at least three ways: in *kind*, in *application*, and in *intensity*.

Consider the example of an adult woman needs to express herself in the world, to make her mark. She might *apply* this by producing saleable or beautiful goods, not by infantile poo-painting, or childish drawings pasted on fridges. She wants to see that her actions make a difference to the world. This is a different *kind* of need than the infant's passive need for general nurturance. The infant wants to feel his mere passive presence makes a difference to the world.

But that general need for appreciation seems to be of the same kind in infants and in adults. Only the area of *application* and the *intensity* seem different.

Brian Schwimme, in his splendid book "The Universe Is A Green Dragon" suggests that a main function of a parent is "to delight in the child". From the child's side, this suggests a very early and primal need to be delighted in and to be seen to be loved – which is an added dimension to, for instance, tactile and nutritional needs.

But the need "to be delighted in", to be appreciated, remains strong in all adults. In babies, there is little we need to do to deserve this delight. In adulthood, we generally have to *be* and to *do* a lot more to get delighted in. Our achievements and skills and abilities and our emotional maturities and so on make us whom we are. The unconditional love babies get becomes more conditional in adult life – and rightly so.

For an adult, to expect to be unconditionally loved for almost total passivity is sheer narcissistic regressiveness. The need to be appreciated for one's achievements might or might not be less intense and perhaps satisfied by soft, subtle appreciation. When the need for appreciation, to be delighted in for our achievements is as intense in adulthood as in childhood for our passivity, we are certainly in a regressed state.

If we feel we could "throw our toys out of the cot" as adults for lack of appreciation of what we do, we are probably regressed. This is how there is a complex overlap of adult life with infantile life. (And that explains why this author is having so much difficulty and frustration in wanting to give his readers a clear idea of what adult love looks like in distinction to infantile love, and is about to throw *his* toys out of the cot!)

THE INTENSITY OF NEED-FULFILMENT

There certainly seem to be quite a few needs of early infancy which, in describing them generally, we would say apply all the way to adulthood, and even unto death — needs for basic acceptance, trust, safety generally and safety from abandonment, belongingness, appreciation for one's uniqueness, and so on. They can all be seen as part of the complex process called "bonding".

I referred earlier to Maslow and Erikson, two psychologists who outlined a list of ages or stages of human maturation. But even they realised that some of the concerns of the earlier stages might live on into the later stages, though no longer be dominant there.

If I have read Maslow correctly, his suggestion is that the lower needs are met by us from the outside, and by others, whereas the higher needs come out of us, and are expressed from our insides out — in growing up, we need to actualise ourselves, express our true selves, fulfil our inner potentials.

This is hard to do if we don't have the basic sense of being delighted in, of trust in the world, of having no fear of abandonment or of rejection. We must have an inner sense of all these things, a basic sense of our own uniqueness, and not, as mature adults, need others or society to give us assurance of these things at every point of our life activities.

If, by the time we are adult, we *don't* have this inner sense of our own self-esteem, appreciation and self-love, a sense of our own uniqueness, and so forth, we may indeed, narcissistically, try to get these from others. The intensity, or over-reaction of our responses, when totally rejected, or totally delighted in, will suggest to us the degree of our regressiveness.

These needs must be fulfilled to a great degree in infancy and then in childhood. That is to say, we need at first to get them from mother and then our nurturing environment generally. *If we have been inadequately fulfilled, we will, as adults, continue looking outside of ourselves for this fulfilment.* And the deepest and most intense forms of this neediness will find expression in intimate love and Soul-mate-seeking. Popularly, we are told, we must "find these things in ourselves, not look to find them from others". This is easier said than done, but is an important truth.

The trouble is that many folk give validity to a different "method" of solving those life problems — by "the method" of falling in love. Because, after all, "love conquers all", or is meant to. But general wisdom in psychotherapy theory suggests we cannot readily, appropriately and properly fill up those unmet childhood needs by getting them fulfilled by another. *We cannot expect our lover, our partner, to "re-parent" us — to give us the perfect infancy and childhood we never had!*

The general approach of psychotherapists is that we must go through grief about all those things we feel we did not receive from our parents generally. In this way we will be able to stop blaming them, and to pop up after our grief and realise we are still okay, that we can put the past in the past, and get on with our present and future lives — not be hung up in the past.

So it is true that as adults we should be looking more into ourselves for having self-love, self-esteem, a sense of our own uniqueness, security about not being abandoned, and so forth. But this does not eliminate entirely the adult need that a certain part of these needs are still desired to be fulfilled from the outside. We still need to feel we are loved, attached, bonded, and deeply appreciated, that our uniqueness is acknowledged, our role in the group honoured, and so forth. These needs never go away entirely. But the levels of desperation about them might vary enormously.

The more we have found these things in ourselves, the less vulnerable we are to any one person or group which frustrates or denigrates us.

FULFILLING NEEDS OR ELIMINATING OUR DESIRES

Whether we are talking about regressive needs or more adult-level needs, there are those in society (often Buddhists) who state that we should *eliminate our needs altogether*, give up our desires, because it is *desires* which make us miserable, vulnerable, and prone to hate people who do not satisfy those desires. Giving up our desires means we will always feel secure, happy, and always able to respect all human beings no matter what they do to us or for us.

We will never call some "good" because they fulfil our needs, or call others "bad" because, simply by being who they are, they intentionally or unintentionally frustrate our needs. In that way we can truly love others, and not expect them to fulfil any of our needs. We can truly give love, and not expect to receive it.

In the romantic domain, however, that yearning, pleasurable ache of desire is validated as something to be gratefully endured —whether fulfilled or not. (And woe to those who have not had the fortune to experience this agonizing, pleasurable pain!)   Certainly in our modern, free-expression Western society, this ache of desire is deemed to be fulfillable, needing only (so goes the folk wisdom) time and patience. According to this mode of thought, only the mate who most deeply evokes desire and most widely satisfies our needs is the one we can really, truly love. The one we *desire* the most is deemed to be the one we *love* the most, whether or not they have any interest in fulfilling our desires or not.

Notice how so much of the identity of potential "Soul Mates" is rooted in whether they can or cannot evoke needs in me, and in whether they desire, or not, to be the fulfiller of my needs — on how much I feel desire for them, and how much of that desire is actually fulfilled freely by them.

Here there is precious little of the element of friendship, and a surplus of narcissism.

Fulfilling of needs creates happiness; but not all needs are fulfillable.

Whenever I find people discussing this topic there seems to be a total dichotomy of possibility —either we both satisfy our desires, and justify that satisfying or seeking to satisfy; or we discredit our desires and needs, and seek to deactivate or restrict or control them. For those wanting to follow the highly disciplined Buddhist path, they will practice the control or even elimination of desire.

I feel a more middle-of-the-road philosophy that makes more sense for most of us Westerners is this: Fulfilling of needs creates happiness; but not all needs are fulfillable!

Neediness which gets too desperate needs serious looking at! *More desperate* means *more regressed* — that is, more evoking of childhood wounds and pains. Whether recognised or not by the lovers, the need-fulfiller is "bigger" and the needy one is "smaller".There is an emotional inequality. Seeing more than there really is, we react more strongly — inevitably we over-react.

I believe it is totally reasonable to seek to satisfy as many needs as we can in our intimate relationship. But if our neediness comes from a desperation that seeks to *consume* the other person, this is a serious regressive dependent state. That is to say; a healthy mature love would involve need-fulfilment for needs which are not in a state of unflinching desperation. In mature love, emotional dependence on the other person has grown from a regressive dependence to an adult dependence, from a relationship of emotional un-equals, to a relationship of equals (as I defined these in terms of "big" and "small" in the chapter on dependence).

Here the other is not *obligated* to fulfil our needs, and he/she is not "wrong" for not fulfilling us. Certainly there is no attempt to *control* the other to make sure they fulfil our needs.

Thus there is no reason for mature love not to have joy from need-fulfilment. But there is every reason for a mature lover not to be in a state where need-frustration leads to reactive pain, aggression, conflict, expectation and force, or emotional devastation or manipulation. So mature love means to be capable of having joy from need-fulfilment, but not necessarily desperate pain from need-frustration — that is, to be capable of *tolerating* need-frustration when it is in any way appropriate to do so. To love truly, we need to drop the expectation that our partner *should* fulfil needs unfulfilled in bad childhoods, or only partially fulfilled in normal childhoods. (152)

The sentence "I want you, but I don't need you" perhaps describes some of that spirit. And certainly, mature love does not label the other person as "bad" for not satisfying a certain need of ours. A French quote suggests that "Love is born of freedom".

Certainly this all makes sense in terms of the origin of the meaning of the word "need", which is related to the Dutch word *nood* and the German *Not* — meaning "danger" or "emergency". Etymologically, this suggests that a need *must* be fulfilled, and that there is *danger* when it won't be fulfilled. Indeed, for the infant, it is dangerous and damaging in many ways when certain needs are not fulfilled. But for an adult, some of those emotional needs should no longer feel so desperate as to be "dangerous" if they are not fulfilled. When, in adults, such need-fulfilment is so desperate, and such needy people feel they have a right to have such needs fulfilled by any means, we get crimes, violence, even murder.

> So mature love means to be capable of
> having joy
> from need-fulfilment,
> but not necessarily desperate pain
> from need-frustration.

End of Narcissism overcome

OVERCOMING THE OTHER ELEMENTS

From Dependence to Uniqueness

Overcoming

2. Dependency

Real, mature love requires that we have, at least to an adequate extent, overcome our small-big emotional dependencies. (Earlier, I distinguished these from factual dependencies). This means we have reached a level of emotional independence where our neediness on others, and especially on our loving partner, is not desperate, not too intense, or over-reactive.

> Real love would require me to give you a helping hand, to help you grow and develop and become independent, and less needy of me. If you still choose me, you will be doing it with a greater degree of freedom, rather than out of a chained, unfree neediness.

As I suggested under the heading of Narcissism above, emotional needs satisfied are not at all a bad thing unless there is desperation about those needs being met. It does mean we both become "equal size" or at least "big enough" in relation to each other emotionally — that we start relating adult to adult.

But in the areas where either of us might still be "small", and still feel needy in relation to the other's "big", the appropriate attitude requires that we do not *expect* our partners to make us safe, and *blame* them when we are not.

IF I AM "SMALL" IN RELATION TO "BIG"

There is a big difference between satisfying my neediness through you and remaining dependent on you as opposed to getting support from you about my neediness in order to help me grow less needy of you. It *does* require me to be able to show my vulnerability and neediness, yet not to validate being rescued in such a way by you that I remain dependent on you.

IF I AM "BIG" IN RELATION TO "SMALL"

And if I am "Mrs Big" in relation to your "small", that is, if you are needy of me, and thus dependent on me, then real love, true love from me, does not consist in my keeping you dependent on me — that would constitute giving-to-get, and would speak of a hidden vulnerability in me.

No! Real love would require me to give you a helping hand up, to help you grow and develop and become independent, and less needy of me. If you still choose me, you will be doing it with a greater degree of freedom, rather than out of a chained, unfree neediness. Then our mutual satisfaction will be big-to-big, adult-sized need satisfaction.

This is all to say there is nothing wrong with dealing with emotional dependency of the small-to-big type in any intimate relationship as long as it is seen as something which must be surpassed, grown beyond. Rescuing someone is best done by giving them the tools and skills and insights that help them to develop their own powers to get themselves out of whatever hole they are stuck in, whatever difficult and painful state they cannot find a way out of.

THE "SMALL-BIG" LESSONS FROM RIVALS IN LOVE

I have already spoken about rivals in love appearing as very "big". There are lessons to be learned where our partner shows such an interest or attachment to a third person. If it is a person we have previously known as "ordinary-sized", and that same person becomes extremely "big" in our eyes, and we feel threatened, we have a handle on our own insecurities, which enables us to realize a needed area of our own psychological growth.

We should even thank the rival for offering us this insight into our own needed area of growth — insight into own area where we have a sense of insecurity!

The following are three vitally important points about our regressive, needy sides:

1. Do not *validate* your own (or your partner's) needs by seeking fulfilment for them
2. Do not *expect* your partner to fulfil them (and do not expect yourself to fulfil them for your partner)
3. Do not *blame* your partner for not fulfilling them (and do not let him/her blame you for not fulfilling them)

This does not imply lack of understanding and compassion towards each other for our past wounds, or even for our normal lack of development. It does mean not validating the regressiveness. It means deciding for ourselves to heal, encouraging our partner to heal, to develop and to grow up to adulthood and beyond, to wisdom and increased pleasure and peace and happiness and excitement.

Real love, in short, does *not* consist in trying to be "unconditionally loving", and inappropriately fulfilling our partner's regressive needs, or making them safe. Real love means a patient encouragement and support for their growing up, growing beyond their regressiveness, beyond their "un-wholeness", beyond their childish wounds, toward a mature independence, leading to a mature, factual, non-needy dependence on a loving partner.

The following are three vitally important points about our regressive, needy sides:
- Do not *validate* needs by seeking fulfilment for them
- Do not *expect* your partner to fulfil them
- Do not *blame* your partner for not fulfilling them

3. The Holding of Boundaries

A state of "no boundaries between us", of "I don't know where you begin and I end" cannot seriously be validated as being a matured state of "true love" or "true romance". And the discovery of boundaries between us, of discovering our separate identities, our differences, cannot seriously be designated as an obstacle to real love, as a problem area of a relationship.

> Clearly, the whole world cannot have changed one iota just because I am in a different mood. It is simply my perception, my perspective which has changed.

If we are to have a relationship that is psychologically an adult-to-adult relationship, as opposed to being psychologically a baby-mother relationship, it means knowing ourselves as deeply as we can, and coming to our intimate relationship with all that we are. After all, if intimacy = "into-me, see", then I must at the least be open to showing myself, and at the most, be always prepared to present the deepest and most authentic parts of me confidently upfront.

The extreme "positivity" and pleasure of the merged state should not be mistaken for true love, for "the real thing!" This state of being merged, of not knowing "where I end and you begin" may be valid as a small part of a relationship, or a temporary part, but ultimately the knowing of exactly whom you are, where you begin and end, and the presenting exactly of who I am, where I begin and end, must be a vital outcome of true love. Here, we simply cannot avoid the truth that in our authenticity we simply cannot have a perfect fit, that we are different, and therefore will have "differences". Can we delight in some of those differences? Can we resolve the conflicts for the differences we have problems with?

We cannot have true love without truth. If we cannot create love between me as I truly am and you as you truly are, we do not have the highly prized "true love".

The issue of what causes the world being either a good or bad, pleasurable or painful place, is not exactly comprehended at early infancy because the infant has no clear idea yet about its own boundaries — where the border is between mother and I. As baby, I am so merged that I don't quite know where I begin and where mother ends. Thus when I am feeling bad, the whole world is a bad place; when I am feeling good, the whole world is a good place. Well, as many of us know, when someone (or ourselves) is in love, the whole world begins to look like a wonderful place, a brighter place, a friendlier place, a place where issues are solved easily or laughed at, etc. etc. That same lack of boundaries seems to occur to the cockeyed optimist in love —not seeing that concurrently with my flighty love and exuberance some people around me may be seriously distressed, anxious, and perhaps even jealous of me, and so on. Clearly, the whole world cannot have changed one iota just because I am in a different mood. It is simply my perception, my perspective which has changed. Like in the womb, like the early infant, myself and the world "are one". It takes

82

just a modicum of adult insight to come to realise that when I am incredibly happy, my partner may not be; when I am incredibly depressed, my partner may not be. We are separate.

Overcoming Of Ambivalence

I suggested earlier that the finding of "true love" feels like the final overcoming of mixed feelings, and that is a highly pleasurable state. "At last I have no mixed feelings about the person I love and want to be with forever."

However, if it is true that mixed feelings (ambivalence) is of the very nature of *all* relationships, *not only intimate relationships*, then mixed feelings will *inevitably* surface.

I suggested that the feeling of falling so deeply in love that one feels one has overcome mixed feelings forever is very often a regressive phenomenon — a feeling of having re-created the bliss of a perfect bond as it was with mother when I was an infant. The feelings of "good" are "exceptionally good", highly pleasurable, greatly satisfying.

Finding the many positive qualities in what initially seems negative requires the skill of love and appreciation. Being ready to see the negatives in what appears at first to be very positive requires the readiness to engage with truth, to refuse to be in denial. Love and truth need to be combined.

The specific emotional tone we are reverting to in romantic love is the one that recreates the times of perfect-fit blissful union with mother — a state of complete non-ambivalence. That is why one of the great joys of romantic love is that it overcomes (albeit temporarily) the pains of having ambivalent feelings as an adult, by recreating the non-ambivalent, blissful times as an infant. "There is only One I love, and that is mum" is what the baby feels. The adult, reliving these experiences in romantic love, feels: "There is only one I love, and that is my partner. I will now love fully. I am totally committed to this relationship. I have no mixed feelings. And I will love this person this way forever."

I feel sure that this is the origin on the romantic adult's "happily ever after" fantasy when discovering "true love" (un-ambivalent love). It is a regression to that timelessness of early life with mother. Hence the fairy tales, which start with a "once upon a time" and end with a "happily ever after", although the story period itself is fraught with many scary or painful challenges.

Note that in these romantic fairy tales these challenges are almost inevitably *external* to the star-struck lovers — their love is depicted as pure and holy and unambivalent, and it is only the world, and folk *outside* them, and *circumstances*, which are trying to prevent them from being together. Think of Romeo and Juliet from Shakespeare, and Tony and Maria in the musical *West Side Story*. Their love is pure and unambivalent. Only society outside of them is trying to prevent their love. Society thus creates a great context for them to prove the strength of their love.

Buts readers who have patiently followed me up to this point might opine otherwise!

> So I suggest it is not just the painful we are escaping from with romantic love, but the complex.

But it is precisely in the "they lived happily ever after" period that the *internal* challenge to their relationship will arise — their ambivalence for each other. When the only challenge is designated in a fairy tale as *external* to the pure love, then the hero or heroine can prove their love by exceptional bravery or gigantic effort to cover distance and overcome obstacles. The "saved" partner shows her ever-faithful love by assurances that the efforts of the hero will be rewarded, that she will remain true to her "saviour". No "darn it! I wish I'd been saved by someone else. Perhaps better looking!"

Therefore romantic fairy tales, in order to keep up the illusion of such non-ambivalent, perfect love and desire, cut off the story line precisely before such an unwanted occurrence as ambivalence will occur. The couple in the romantic story can only love each other as long as there are challenges from *outside*. Once they have to settle down and live together, how to create life and loveliness and delight becomes a different story altogether. The "monster" that the hero and/or heroine have to fight is now their own ambivalence. And the problem now becomes: how to create love in the suburbs *without* the world outside providing great challenges in trying to prevent that?

HERE IS MY THEORY ABOUT ALL THIS: In finding such perfect-fit love we are not only trying to escape the pain of ambivalence, but the reality of *MULTIVALENCE* — that our lives and loves are far more complex than simply "good and/or bad". In fact, there is often bad *in* the good, and good *in* the bad.

I suggest that both the "good" and the "bad" infantile perspectives are very primitive mid and lower-brain functions — the sort of brain functions that humans have which enable them to divide the world into "this" and "that", "them" and "us", "good" and "bad", "friend" and "enemy". It is a failure to acknowledge and engage with the truth that people – both us and our partners – are far more complex than that, and that nothing about us can so easily be divided into simplistic "goods" and "bads" (which is precisely what the yin-yang sign, discussed below, implicitly suggests).

This means, that the good is not necessarily *all* good, and the bad not necessarily *all* bad, "but thinking makes it so" (as the famous Shakespeare quote from Hamlet suggests). Actually, it is not "thinking" that makes it so. It is more because every single aspect of a person takes place within the greater context of the whole person — thus a person lazy in one area of his life may be so because of being overworked in another area. And often, in relationships, it takes time and skill to realize these things, to see the same things from a different perspective, against a different background. And this may make us realize that what we thought was weak, is actually strong; what we saw as ugly, is actually beautiful; what we saw as dysfunctional, actually has a value we were incapable of seeing at the time. The inherently lazy person may be more in touch with his body's needs for rest and health than the energetic person, who may be burning himself out by firing his furnace too hot. The "lazy" person might end up living long, and the high-burning person might develop cancer or heart disease and die young.

"Ambi" means "both", and "valent" means "of worth, of value". "Ambi-valence", accordingly, implies a *binary* state. What we need to realize instead is a state of *Multi-Valence*. We need to realise that there is a *complexity* of values, and that the same human quality can look strong from one point of view, weak from another, positive from one viewpoint, negative from another.

This notion of *complex multivalence* versus the *simpler ambivalence* correlates well with what we know about how the brain functions. The lower and mid-brain sections fire in terms of either/or (binary) functions: fight or flight, approach or avoid, etc. etc. These primitive parts of the brain only know over-simplified stimuli, to which they react strongly.

85

One might even say they **over-react.**

The higher brain, the cortex, lives in a very complex world, where "yes" vs "no" is not quite so simple, where "good" vs "bad" is not so clearly defined, because there are pros and cons on each side.

And the higher brain also enables us to press our "pause" button!

Pressing the "pause" button is *required* to avoid the limitations of the lower brain functions, the binary, simplistic brain sections with their too-too quick decisions in situations that require slower, more thought-out, felt-out, sensed-out, intuited-out, deliberated decisions.

Our neo-cortex, our higher-brain functions, our fine human intellects, enable us, if we allow ourselves to, to see that anything which we are ready to label as "bad" might have positive aspects, and anything we might label as "good" might have negative aspects. Finding positive qualities in what initially seems negative requires the skill of love and appreciation. Being ready to see the negatives in what appears at first to be positive requires the readiness to engage with truth, to refuse to be in denial.

Love and truth need to be *combined.*

Complex ambivalence (i.e. multivalence) means for us that the world is a complex and difficult place. It is difficult to make decisions — *all* involve loss or compromise. It is much easier to see the world as black or white. That way we can guarantee that we *feel* intensely, and *think* minimally (which is what makes us the dumb humans we often are —not integrating the complex elements of these two).

This might be easier for us. But it is simplistic, limiting, denigrative, and fails to honour the real complexity of the world and of others. After all, *nobody and nothing* satisfies us *totally*, and they are not bad for being so. By the same token, when we *do* feel totally satisfied in romance, a temporary state, does it really mean that our lover is totally good, or necessarily better than anyone else?

I suggest, then, it is not just the frustrating and painful we are escaping from with romantic love, but the *complex.*

For the truth is that romantic love is the illusion which over-simplifies the real complexity of life, thereby initially seeming to overcome the pains and difficulties of having to negotiate the reality of our complex, inevitably incompatible natures.

A "compatibility of incompatibles" is what real adult intimacy is ultimately about.

Romantic illusion is easier, less stressful, and avoids conflict. But it also wipes out the richness of the real complexity of our lives. The reason is that in the complex multivalent world we are more aware of causality, of what *really* causes what. And this removes the childish magic of the world, the sense of things happening mysteriously and wondrously. We know "how the magician performs the trick" and this makes the whole show "boring". But it is especially "boring" if all we are seeking is "magic" in relationships. And if we are incapable of making magic and gleaning joy from the ordinary.

When ambivalence re-surfaces in a "perfect-fit" relationship, many Soul-Mate-Seekers and incurable romantics think that they have made a terrible mistake of judgment, and immediately want leave that relationship. They want to go back to, to re-find, a pre-ambivalent state of perfect-fit beautiful blissful bonding.

Well, in some situations, perhaps it *is* time to leave. But in others, it is time to wake up and grow up — to look at how we *ourselves* cut off relationships which might *still* have enormous potential.

And part of this might be discovering that what annoyed us in the past was our own unjustified judgmentalism. Similarly, what delighted us was our neediness in a certain area. But with time, the annoyance and delight might disappear for those particular areas, while arising in others, and we might have to move on to new ways at looking at and delighting in our partner — part of the skill of love as an art.

THAT ILLUSORY YIN-YANG SYMBOL
The age-old yin-yang symbol provides a good illustration of the reduction of the complexity of life and love to two simplistic binary parameters which fit each other perfectly — an appropriate symbol of blissful bonding.

The satisfaction of important needs creates for us the feeling of a perfect fit with our partner, and lovers have for ages used the yin-yang symbol as an expression of their love, although it comes from a much wider metaphysical tradition.

Encyclopaedia Britannica tells us:

> *In the 3rd century BCE in China, it formed the basis of an entire school of cosmology (the Yinyang school), whose main representative was Zou Yan." (131)*

It has been used for such abstract forces as heaven and earth, and masculinity and femininity.

But let me point out an elusively obvious limitation of this. The yin-yang symbol reduces complex multi-dimensionality to a simple two-dimensional form. For instance, all the things which make up "heaven" are fitted together with all the things which make up "earth", and so Heaven and Earth become perfectly related in the yin-yang symbol. Heaven, for instance, provides rain and sun, and earth provides nourishing chemicals for plants, so, judging only by these criteria, heaven and earth fit together perfectly. But here we have reduced both the idea of heaven and the idea of earth to simplistic dimensions.

Now, no matter what your political or philosophical or religious or spiritual leanings, the happenings on earth, and the happenings in heaven, are pretty complex, and far from simplistically one- or two-dimensional.

Climatically speaking, the heavens burn large swathes of the earth into deserts, completely flood other areas, cause droughts and tsunamis, as well as doing the most splendid things like helping our crops grow, and flowers to bloom, and generally helping us to prosper. In religion, the heavens are seen as consisting in many different and complex moral systems, instructions from God, or the gods, and can in no way be accurately represented as a 2-dimensional, simple form as in the yin-yang symbol.

So, in order to reduce heaven and earth to only two dimensions, one would have to choose some simple aspect of what happens on earth and match it up with an equally simple aspect of what we assume is the nature of heaven. There's a name for this process: *over-generalisation.*

Yes, the sun *does* make the flowers grow. But it *also* often burns crops to death. The principle applies to *any* two things which have many parts, and a complex structure. Take any such objects and try and squeeze them together to form a perfect fit — say a car and motorcycle: they won't mesh. You *could* mould the car door to take in the motorbike's petrol tank, and that would be a perfect fit — but only by doing violence to each "partner" in the "equation".

What I am trying to say is that the yin-yang idea as applied to human lovers takes two complex beings, and reduces them to two parts which just happen to fit together perfectly – but only, as in the example above, by doing violence to each partner in the equation.

To me, the longevity and power of such symbols as the yin-yang is a testament to regressive fantasies of perfect bonding which humans have nurtured all through history. We have always longed for the perfect "mother and child reunion", have always desired the elusive perfect fit.

The beautiful Gustav Klimt paintings that depict a man and a woman, each in beautiful garb, snuggling perfectly into each other's bodies, amount very much to this same yin-yang image. They represent a perfect fit of two static images which can only represent a tiny fraction of the moving, living lives of the two people in the relationship.

Paint them having a disagreement about how to bring up the kids, and that would be a different picture altogether. But note that this would *also* represent only a single moment in time. A moment in time which simply cannot capture the moving, ongoing life of real, live humans being and doing.

I recently saw a Soul Mate card, saying "I finally found you, my missing puzzle piece". Now missing puzzle pieces, once you find them, fit together perfectly.

And that is just another form of the "yin-yang" message.

> Yet the longevity and power of such symbols as the Yin-Yang is a testament to regressive fantasies of perfect bonding which humans have nurtured all through history.

At this point I would like to propose what I consider a more realistic symbol of a connection between two full and real human beings. This connection would *include* areas where lovers *conflict* with each other, *where the fit does not seem so perfect*. And it would also include areas where we *fail* to connect, or where in fact we have *no need to connect at all* — where we are quite happy living *separate* lives, with no ensuing problems. (I hope the Reader will forgive me for having a quiet, private giggle about having created a symbol which suggests serious "work" and, quite literally, "coming to grips" with the "nuts and bolts" of relationships!)

THE PLIERS SYMBOL

A MORE REALISTIC "YIN-YANG" SYMBOL

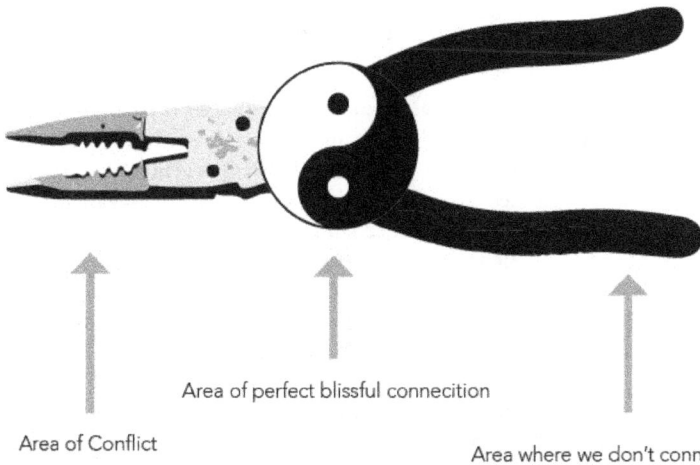

Area of perfect blissful connecition

Area of Conflict

Area where we don't connect at all

89

To summarise, then – I believe that, like the yin-yang sign, the perfect-fit strategy of Soul-Mate-Seekers and Incurable Romantics reduces the complexity of the natures of two real people, the "multivalence", to an over-simplistic two-parts-fitting-perfectly-together, a recreation of mother-child bliss.

This strategy fails to deal with reality. We are complex creatures, and there *are* no easy and perfect fits. Hence we have to *deal* with our incompatibilities in intimate relationships, to *find* ways to make those work, to resolve conflict, and so on.

THE ISSUE OF COMPROMISE

The issue of compromise in intimate relationships is also relevant here. One of this author's radical stances about real love is that *it does not need compromise*. But we must make a distinction here. There are two different ways of accepting that certain needs won't be fulfilled, two different ways of compromising.

"Bad Compromise" is when we feel we are losing out by giving in, by not having our way, by not having what we want. This kind of compromise is bound to make us feel diminished.

"Good Compromise", on the other hand, is when, by giving up something, and giving in to something, we gain something *else*, something *larger, wider, more important*. When we can learn to make compromises for a greater good, there is a feeling of expansiveness, of gaining rather than losing. So this kind of compromise is not problematic.

Good Compromise works best when we can take in the perspective of the other, give it full validity, and perhaps even feel we could adopt it as our own. We then feel enriched by the other person rather than impoverished.

5. Overcoming the Expectation of Magic

Perhaps the most useful thing I can say about the experience or the expectation of magic early in romantic phases of relationships is that one should "press the pause button on it" — in other words, wait to see how real or general it is. There is probably a big difference between magic that occurs too easily and spontaneously, and magic that is produced from the adult skills of life and relating which have been honed consciously over years.

That is to say, magic that comes from "feelings" or "vibes" about the other person that one cannot quite put one's finger on, and cannot quite describe, might be a regressed magical bond. Some of this magical view of love was expressed in Joni Mitchell's 1969 hit song "Both Sides Now". It talks of the romance of moons and Ferris wheels, of the magical dizziness we feel when fairy tales become real, and of how the singer has looked at love that way, "from only one side". (157)

A different matter is the magic that one feels in appreciating the other's real adult skills. We could distinguish two areas of such skills. Firstly, those due to education, training, etc. Secondly, those involved in communication, in "emotional intelligence", in how we resolve conflicts, in being kind and in being intimate, and so on, as we grow up. In this area, some people are more skilled than others. Note that communication skills are honed over a lifetime, and are specific to good bonding. If, despite being weak in any of these areas, you still find a spontaneous, magical connection with someone because "we seem to be on the same 'vibration'", I would caution against being too quick to validate such magic.

And of course, romantic love does flood the body with all kinds of "mind-altering" substances – adrenalin, dopamine, oxytocin, serotonin, and so on. These, no doubt, enhance the illusion of a magical emotional connection, as well as producing inexhaustible energy to show that we are great need-fulfillers to the object of our love.

In the romantic phase, ambivalence has not yet been re-discovered, and this allows us to believe in *magic*, rather than real-world *causality*. And, crucially, the romantic phase makes us forget *how much skill, knowledge, and energy the real world, not to mention real-world relationships, demand.*

When ambivalence inevitably surfaces in relationships, this is followed by exchanges about "who did what for whom?" and "how much?" or "how little?" In other words, we get to the question of "who broke the magic bond?" But this should not lead to blame, or even disappointment.

To manifest *real* love, we have to manifest it in the *real* world, not the *magical* world. Over the course of a relationship, we inevitably discover areas where we are not spontaneously compatible and "magical". But thus we know each other better as real persons.

Can't we make something of these "differences"? Can't we *make* love, where previously we merely *found* love? Can't we move beyond the infantile regressed state of expecting magical connections based on simplistic, limited parts of each other? Can't we move on to an adult-world connection to the real complexity of another human being?

In the adult world, the things that are *really magical* are the amazing skills that individuals have honed over years, so as to produce things for us that we are totally incapable of producing. These skills we experience as magic, be they practical skills, or relationship skills.

For sometimes we fall in love with others who are in effect actualising parts of ourselves which we wish we ourselves could actualise. In this, the other person seems magical, and we are enthralled. But a mistake many people make is that, in order to possess this skill vicariously, they think they must *have this other person as a partner.*

I think a worthwhile question is this: "Shouldn't I also try to actualize myself as you have, and develop in myself the ability I so admire in you? Because you are a perfect symbol of my unactualised aspects? You show me what I could be if I were to be my best self."

In other words, a better approach is to *become* what one so admires in the other — *if* that is genuinely what one wants to achieve in life. The sense of the magical-ness of the other will then become more normalised, and the need for the other will be lessened – but not necessarily the love. What I originally loved in you as an ability, I now love in both of us.

Another way of putting this: I have found in *myself* the magic I was looking for and seeing in *you*.

Now I love us both.

6. Beyond Simplistic Uniqueness

There is nothing unique about uniqueness.

The stress on searching for "The One" who will be so unique as to be perfect-fitting in every way is based on the fantasy that we shall automatically find someone where our ambivalence, our mixed feelings will spontaneously evaporate, forever. This is a regressive fantasy — the fantasy of the "perfect-fit" partner.

As I noted when discussing the yin-yang symbol, we are complex creatures. And *two complex creatures can only bond together perfectly when they bond with just a part of their being.* The unique bond created by meshing only a small section of two complex whole beings must, by its very nature, constitute a very simple uniqueness. A few parts fit, but of course most don't.

I am suggesting that the simplistic uniqueness we find in each other when we fall in love is *inevitably* limited, because we simply do not know each other well, and it takes time for more of our personalities to emerge and show themselves.

But I also suggest that this simplistic uniqueness we feel and discover in each other is inevitably a regressed uniqueness. For one thing, in the bliss-bunny phase, there is no ambivalence, hence only positive-part matches between us are seen. Perhaps, if the bond feels "ineffable", "indescribable", "mysterious", this in itself is further proof of its regressiveness — of a reversion to the pre-verbal bond with mother.

Interestingly enough, real adult uniqueness, based on adult qualities, not on "feelings", "sensations", "moods" or "vibes", *can be described more easily and specifically* — "what I love about her is . . . ".

And in adult reality we are more likely to know that there are areas we are ambivalent about, and ultimately, that we are dealing with the multivalence which is simply inseparable from the nature of intimate relationship between two very complex beings.

I said earlier that there is nothing unique about uniqueness. But remember that we have a tendency to regard our partner's uniqueness, or our unique bond, as special. We "special-ize" our uniqueness, thinking it is way better and finer that the uniqueness of *other* people's bonds, or the uniqueness of *other* people's partners. I think this is a kind of narcissism. It is a disrespect for the uniqueness of other people, other lovers, devaluing their bond below ours.

A famous Tina Turner song proclaims that "you are simply the best ... better than all the rest". Well, while you might be the best fit for *me*, that certainly does not make you superior to other lovers who are the best fit for *their* particular partners.

Another famous song, this time by Leonard Cohen, suggests, however, that our love is similar to the love of all other lovers in the world (words slightly changed):

> *Many have loved before us. We simply are not new.*
> *In cities and in forests, they smile like me and you*

"I thought you were different from other women/men" is sheer fantasy.
I *am* different!
But I also have certainly commonalities which I share with all those of my gender.

The issue of being too focussed on finding and keeping the most unique partner (as the highest expression of love) inherently contains in it another conundrum which must be addressed in all relationships: that all intimate relationships have many things in common with each other. Therefore the dramas being played out, the issues being resolved and so forth, are often universal issues, or at least common to a whole society, culture, or nation. I think we very often tend to downplay these universal challenges to all relationships when we get too romantic, and too "Soul-mate-seeking".

"I thought you were different from other women/men" is sheer fantasy. I *am* different! But I also have certainly commonalities which I share with all those of my gender. So part of the story of our relationship is not just a story of extreme uniqueness, but a playing out of the story of common human nature in these matters of our very human attempts at intimacy.

I am not denying the importance of searching for, and finding, a partner with a certain amount of special (that is "specialized" by you, uniquely!) uniqueness — a uniqueness which we find spontaneously, and enjoy with special affection. We might, in the early romantic period, feel we have found such a special uniqueness that we now have our perfect-fit partner.

But as I have tried to show, we all find, over time, the imperfectly fitting areas. And these are in reality the glorious areas where we can seriously meet and engage with the real and valid differences of our partner. These are the areas where we now have the challenge to *make* love where none might have existed before. These are the areas where we discover *"the Other" rather than "the One"*.

We might even say we discover the "otherness", and unhook from the idea of our "one-ness". In this way we might discover a cornucopia of richness born of the complexity of the relationship, rather than an intensity of blissful bonding based on limited, simplistic ties.   Actually, it is not quite accurate to speak of "*The* Other". Instead, we ought to speak of "*One* Possible Other". For in fact *there are several "theoretical" others with whom we are capable of creating love and intimacy*. There are around us, if we can find them, an adequate set of beings with unique-enough qualities we can enjoy, each slightly different from the other, but with whom we can decide to connect in exclusive, committed relationships, to en-joy (give and get joy from) and decide to try and *make* love and intimacy with.

7. Beyond "Love at First Sight"

At this stage of the book, I hope I do not need to say much about the dangers of the notion of love at first sight. Very occasionally people *do* successfully follow up love at first sight with successful long-term relationships. But mostly there is simply a blindness to the other issues and problems of life and love beyond the romantic phase. And, of course, a blindness to the almost inevitable possibility of regressiveness, and thus copious misperception occurring right now in the present.

At "first sight", we are dealing with a very vague stimulus. I suggested that when we look at a vague stimulus, what we see there tends to be more formed by something inside us than what we actually see out there in the other. In short, we are *projecting*.

But, if we don't realise that we are doing this, we will certainly think we "can see very clearly how I will be with this potential partner, this fabulous person in my sights". But this "seeing clearly" is actually "seeing very unclearly"

— it is a total failure to wait for the "scene" to play itself out more fully, to show more of itself.

If we fail to realise, when we "see things clearly from *inside* ourselves", that we are dealing with a vague stimulus outside of ourselves, we are in danger of a total misperception. Realising that we are dealing with a vague and as yet unknown stimulus gives us the power and intelligence to "press the pause button" and wait for more about this love object to reveal itself in time.

End of
Overcoming the Other Elements
of Regression

VALIDATING OUR REGRESSIVENESS

The Starting Base for the Problem of Regressiveness

VALIDATING OUR REGRESSIVENESS AND EXPECTATIONS

The opening problem is not necessarily that we may be regressed, and because of that misperceive the real nature of our partner, and because of that, in turn, "mis-respond" to the other. Similarly, the starting problem is not that we are wounded (hopefully temporarily, not permanently).

The problem comes when we are *unaware* that we are regressed, or wounded, or under-developed, and *unaware* that we are in need of growing up, healing our wounds, developing our under-developed, weaker areas.

This implies that we are unaware of our misperceptions of the other, of what, because of denial, we might be blind-spotting about the other, and how we might be projecting onto them qualities that are not really there. Thus we "mis-react" and "mis-respond" because the "stimulus" to which we are reacting is a false, confusing stimulus — far more complex than what we first imagined.

The problem is also that, because of our unawareness, we validate, we give credence to, the expectation that all our needs must be fulfilled. This allows us to justify the belief that our *partner* is responsible for how we feel, and we are fully entitled to blame *them* for that. Also, we believe that the magical, spontaneous, beautiful blissful bond that occurs, with its blindness to the reality of both my real nature and my partner's real nature, must go on forever, because we designate this as *True Love*.

When, inevitably, the illusion breaks down, and there is disappointment, and frustration, *the belief* that the regressed states are the real love will keep the lovers in a real downer of a state, perhaps cynical about ever finding or creating real love. There might even be a desire to find a way back to the previous regressed bliss.

Let's see what happens when we give credence to the *elements of regression*:

1. NARCISSISM. If you truly want to hold onto the idea that your partner, (like mother for the baby) is only here for *me*, you might find it hard to realise that they have a life totally separate and distinct from you. If you feel really vulnerable, and feel justified in holding on to the philosophy that your partner should be "only for you", you might try to stop her or him from having some life separate from you. This can turn into abuse, but at the least, into resentment and unjustified disappointment.

2. DEPENDENCE. If your partner was "big" for you, when you were "small", you might want to keep her or him stuck in the all-holding, dependable role, and maintain yourself as "small" and needy. Accordingly, you might feel seriously let-down when the partner cannot be the great bearer of all responsibilities and burdens. If you are "Big", but "Small" grows up and needs you less, you might feel let down, un-needed, vulnerable.

3. BOUNDARIES. In the beginning we did not know where "I ended and you began". Our joy was spontaneous, and it seemed as if the lack of a "skin", a boundary between us did not matter because we were only exchanging nourishing, pleasurable "fluids" with each other. Now that we have discovered that some non-nourishing, and perhaps even poisonous fluids are being exchanged, we realize there *are* boundaries between us, and we want to figure out who is doing what to whom, so that we can know who to blame. Most probably we shall want to blame the Other as the one who destroyed the beautiful blissful bond.

4. AMBIVALENCE. If you validate the pre-ambivalent state of pure pleasure and bliss, then, when ambivalence returns, you will want to find a situation (or perhaps a different partner) where there is only the pleasurable side of things, without problems or pains. Instead of confronting the situation which has both good and bad, pain and pleasure, and moving forward, you might wish to change the situation (or your partner) so that the 'bad' never happens again. But as I have proposed, growth, development and forward movement entail not only dealing with ambivalence, but also confronting the reality of complex multivalence.

5. MAGICAL THINKING. Again, if we expect love to make doves appear out of thin air, we may be sorely disappointed when the magic stops. We have to progress to a new stage where we appreciate that much real "magic" in life is produced by hard-earned skill. And we may have to look deeply into ourselves to find the tools necessary for creating good relationships.

6. UNIQUENESS. We will come to learn that our partner's uniqueness, though very special to us, is not the *only* uniqueness among potential lovers, and that there are *other* unique people too, with different qualities, equally valuable. It might disappoint us to realise that our partner is not as unique in certain areas as *other* people's partners or *other* potential partners. This is especially true if we expect to feel that our partner's uniqueness is special in *all* areas – wider, deeper, higher than the uniqueness of *all* other partners. We need to recognise and love our partner's uniqueness without being blind to the uniqueness of *other* people's partners.

Our partner's uniqueness takes its place as *one uniqueness among many*.

7.   LOVE AT FIRST SIGHT. When we finally recognise the blind spots we may have had when falling in or for love at first sight, this should not send us back to seeking the "earlier glory". It should force us to decide whether to go forward or not with this real person we have just discovered.

Validating our own regressiveness means expecting to have all our needs fulfilled by our partner.

Validating our partner's regressiveness means accepting that we fulfil their needs, and thus validating our guilt feelings if we don't, and validating our egos if we do. But in both cases the onus on fulfilment comes from the other person.

We consider them to be loving when they satisfy our needs, and thus we feel loved.   We consider them unloving when they don't satisfy our needs, and we feel unloved, perhaps even unlovable.

We consider ourselves to be loving when we satisfy their needs, and expect them to feel loved and lovable.

Our desperation to be validated as a loving person gets satisfied when we see that they need us and are getting need-fulfilment from us. But if it is just about stroking our own ego, then it is not real love, for the main concern is for ourselves, not for them.

It is only when we really feel concern for the other and their lives, outside of all our own concerns, that there is real love.

Such concern is not at all rare. Many people do feel this for others. Many people have a natural empathy for the sufferings and needs of others. When fulfilling their needs, we are thinking only about them, not about our own status or about points scored.

But it is when our fulfilling of their needs is more about validating our own value as persons rather than about fulfilling their concerns that the love is *giving-to-get*.

One of the main ways of misperception is by the process of projection. And one of the main causes of over-reaction is such misperception from projecting too strongly, perceiving reality too weakly.

In summary, in the movement from regressive love to mature and adult love the following happens to the elements of regression:

1. <u>Narcissism</u> moves to genuine selfless care for others, without expecting a reward.

2. <u>Dependence</u> moves to a more mature inter-dependence. Love goes from *desperate* need-fulfilment to *calm, patient* need-fulfilment and an absence of desperation and anxiety at need-frustration.

3. We each have very clear <u>boundaries</u> which we hold (even if tentatively) as to who we are and how we are different from, and not merged with, our partner, who has clear boundaries of their own.

4. Our <u>ambivalence</u> is overcome by accepting both "good" and "bad" sides of our partner, but also proceeding to understanding <u>multivalence</u> — that the whole love scene can and should be seen more than just in terms of "black and white" ("good and bad").

5. <u>Magical thinking</u> gets replaced by *the magic of realism* about the efforts of love involved.

6. Seeking <u>unique validation</u> from you gets replaced by me self-validating my own uniqueness, being secure in my own sense of uniqueness. The ability to love, which can be applied generally, non-uniquely, as a skill, becomes an added force in the picture of love. Applying the skill uniquely to this partner creates a unique history to our relationship which is special. Validation of our deep blissful feelings as "real love" gets replaced by the realization that some of those feelings are <u>"over-reactions"</u>.

7. <u>Love at first sight</u> is seen as illusory mainly because it projects perfection, "pure love with no conflicts or problems" onto the potential partner. When you feel "love at first sight", press the "pause button"!

Being Aware Of One's Misperceptions and Over-reactions

What the Elements of Regression all have in common is total misperception of the other person and the situation between them. One of the main ways of misperception is by the process of projection. And one of the main causes of over-reaction is such misperception from projecting too strongly, perceiving reality too weakly.

Something that constantly amazes me is how convinced people are of their own projections, thinking they are seeing reality, and not being able to distinguish whether there are really facts or data to support the truth of what they see from their own imaginings. They see "so very clearly" — because inside themselves they are capable of painting a clear picture of what they *imagine* to be true.

As usual, many love songs vividly describe these psychological processes:

> *I can see us on an April night,*
> *sipping brandy underneath the stars*
> *reading poems in the candlelight...*

> — **from the 1951 musical *Paint Your Wagon***

> **by Lerner and Loewe**

He "sees" very clearly (i.e. projects!) how "we" will be, together, outside on an April night. What he does *not* realize is that she hates the taste of brandy, will catch a chill outside on an April night, and is not particularly interested in poetry. But he has taken the few areas of their pleasurable connection and generalized them into an all-round perfect fit.

I have already referred to the phenomenon of Over-reaction. When I said that the romantic illusion is a *positive* over-reaction to a person or situation, I remind the reader that I was talking about a strong reaction of *extreme bliss* as a possible over-reaction. (Popularly, by contrast, an "over-reaction" is usually *negative*: pain, embarrassment, anger, etc.)

> *Real* love involves a *real* reaction or response to a *real* person accurately perceived.

We need to evaluate if our very intense reactions and feelings are an excessive painting of ideal perfect fit onto the partner, or whether our strong feelings are tempered by clear perception of what is going on, both in ourselves, and in our partner.

Real love involves a *real* reaction or response to a *real* person accurately perceived.

A strong reaction based on clear perception has its own magic, but of a very different kind than regressed magic. This is the "real magic" of people who seem, by their hard work and exceptional skill, to produce "magically" beautiful music and writing, hilarious comedy, infectious energy, marvellous movement and delightful dance, creative solutions, massive productiveness, effective problem-solving, and so on.

In general, all this means we need to be aware that we are almost certainly misperceiving the situation, projecting a perfect bliss and harmony onto it, and pleasurably over-reacting to it because of that.

The blindness about the fact of our regressiveness needs special spectacles to see, and many couples remain blind to these till death do them part. I hope, by writing this book, that I have provided some magnifying-glass power by which we can see these things somewhat more clearly.

To sum up, then – in mature and real love, projections and misperceptions are replaced by seeing other people as they really are, not as we make them up to be. Then the real engagement with a real other adult person begins, with all the joys and problems that those involve.

The engagement with the full story-in-waiting.

 **End of Overcoming the elements Of Regression**

BEING

A

GROWNUP

IN

LOVE

ADULT LOVE

Of course, we do grow up way beyond our second year of life. We slowly become active, speak more and more, and even use our language as a form of action. We become more and more complex, more and more differentiated in high individualism, exceptional uniqueness (*everybody* does!) and eventually gain an adult identity of sorts.

And of course, love and marriage (and all other serious partnerships) are all about adult identity. And there are many developing adult psychological processes which are not touched on in this book, but can be found in the thousands of books written about them and about "how to have a good intimate relationship".

Adult love cannot be about re-creating a wonderful "mother and child reunion" where each of us is nurturing infantile, regressive impulses in the other. The model for adult love cannot be a mother-child bond.

The purpose of this book, uniquely, I think, (says this author, fishing, no doubt, for love and appreciation for his own uniqueness!) is to try to show that some very powerful processes from very early life – pre-verbal, "ineffable" processes, formidable patterns – often remain and are in fact omnipresent in adult love. Some theorists have argued that the good, positive, pleasurable, blissful sides of those early infancy days actually hold an important model worthy of being searched for and re-found in adult love —that the early blissful years hold the golden mould for a shining adult connection. I have argued strongly against this.

As much as it might constitute an enormous advantage to have experienced blissful bonding in early years, it remains a blissful bonding in which there is a *baby* who is intensely dependent on a *mother*. However, *adult* love cannot be about re-creating a wonderful "mother and child reunion" where each of us is nurturing infantile, regressive impulses in the other. The model for adult love cannot be a mother-child bond.

Rather it must be a model of two fully grown adults, totally separate and independent from their childhood carers, now capable of making their own "babies" — two whole adults whose "intercourse" – together with the differences they each bring – makes unique third things, metaphorical "babies" (that is to say, interesting products of their adult union) (191)

> **It means being open to hear what we are normally totally deaf to, seeing what we are normally blind to.**

At any rate, adult intimacy does usually begin with great spontaneous connections. Adult spontaneous connections occur when we fall in love and we find amazing ways in which we can connect with each other, excite each other, stimulate each other with adult qualities which we bring to the relationship.

But we need to test whether these have a regressive emotional element.

Eventually this spontaneous connection excitement winds down. Now we have to learn the skills of making something come alive for the other and for ourselves. And also to be open to letting the other make something come alive for us, stimulating us with something new.

The first requires communication skills involving being able *to express ourselves clearly*. The second requires communication skills which involve *learning to listen*, which ultimately means either to delight in the life of the other, or at least to validate their excitement, or deep meaningfulness, about some different aspect of their life.

It means being open to hear what we are normally totally deaf to, seeing what we are normally blind to.

All the above amounts to the simple truth that having a good relationship involves half *finding love* and half *making love* — that is cooking up some love where some may not at first exist using the best ingredients and the finest recipes. Finding a right, fitting, adult partner involves finding one with the best ingredients for being able to "cook up a storm" (or at least a fine, peaceful meal) together.

This all takes learning, and there is a plethora of excellent literature around for those who earnestly want to understand the ups and downs of love.

The year before I entered university there was a lunchtime lecture there about the psychology of love by a great psychoanalyst. She proposed that "Love is when two people do what only one wants to do, but both end up enjoying it".

That is to say, we each show each other another part of life, from the vast experiences we have learned from, and if we are open to it, can see its significance and enjoy it. We create life for the other. And the other responds deeply to that life that we created for them. And vice versa.

SO WHAT IS REAL LOVE?

Becoming Who We Were Meant to Be

At the very least, real love involves overcoming the regressiveness delineated in this book. Regressive feelings are very powerful, create great blissful excitement, but blind us to the reality of what is before us.

After overcoming regressiveness, we also need to look at conflict resolution. In conflict resolution we need to examine our own contribution to sustaining conflict by holding onto rigidly judgmental stances — that we know "how things are supposed to be". It also involves looking at any other area of ourselves which can be destructive to the relationship. And then we need to look beyond regressiveness and conflict and judgmentalism and destructiveness towards the delightful hills and valleys where we might find real, more mature, more exciting and tastier love.

> But a couple who are not the same in any way might still totally delight in their differences. And a couple who have differences which in no way complement each other can still totally delight in each other.

Partners Support Each Other To Grow And Develop
Partners support each other, especially in areas meaningful to the partner, but not necessarily meaningful to oneself. That is, we acknowledge and feel the significance of what our partner does in life that has no direct advantage or need-fulfilment to ourselves. We delight in *their* growth and development, and see it as an enrichment to both of us, and our family as a whole.

Partners See Each Other Clearly
What this means is that each partner really experiences the meaningful way that the other lives their life and values. They do not see each other's life as meaningless.

This author's impression of many people he meets who are still searching desperately for love, or indeed who have given up in despair about ever finding love, is that they simply do not realise their own narcissism. That is, they do not realise that they are continually expressing themselves with the desperate hope that someone will see them deeply, find them interesting, stimulating. Nevertheless, they have very little interest or time, or listening space, to allow the *other* to express themselves.

But real love means receiving the other person fully in all their reality. And real love and listening abilities mean that we are never without love, because love goes where we go.

Being Good at Conflict Resolution

A good relationship contains two people who are really good at conflict resolution. Conflict resolution has two main branches.

Firstly, one has to stop one's judgmentalism,—the easy and unnecessary put-down of the other for the most petty and insignificant things (In *Falling for Love* I wrote at length on this).

Secondly, one has to be able to appreciate the validity of many values which are totally different to and contradictory of one's own. Let's take a deeper look at this.

Respecting Values Which Are Totally Different From Mine

In this situation, we can truly say "we do not have this in common. Here, we do not complement each other. Neither are we the same, in this regard".

Let's take an example:

> I like holding on to objects found or bought which I consider to be sacred objects in my life, perhaps objects I find incredibly beautiful, or incredibly meaningful, or which hold important memories. These things are sacred to me. The past holds a vital background against which my present and future is figure, from which it is "projected" forward.
>
> My partner is the opposite of me. We have nothing in common on this score. We are not the same, neither do our different ways complement each other. Our different ways clash completely —certainly in the living spaces which we share together. My partner believes in holding onto *absolutely nothing*. For her, sacredness consists of letting go of all and any such attachments, and moving on, beyond the past, beyond memories. For her, memories are just "sentimentality".

In such a situation partners can either totally and continually judge each other as "wrong", as "stupid" *or* can come to understand the validity of the other point of view, that the other side is as valid and in need of respect as our own viewpoint.

If my partner destroys something of mine because she thinks "it is stupid to hold onto things so preciously", she will be disrespecting my values. If I plead with her not to get rid of something that I think is important for her, or will be important in the future, but she insists, I might be failing to see how the world looks from *her* side.

Part of learning mature love, which is about going beyond narcissism, involves being able to listen very carefully to how my partner came to have that particular viewpoint, and how I, if I had walked the same path, in the same moccasins, would have come to the same conclusion.

This is a *skill* that must be learned, practised, developed, in order to be a better lover. It means learning to delight in or at least appreciate a difference which does not enhance one's own standpoint. And often, by understanding how your partner came to his or her point of view, you might even decide to change your own stance and values. Such good listening ability leads to something called 'growing and changing'. And we might note how easily and often we meet people with whom we have a lot in common, but we do not feel desire to have intimate love with them. This is to say, just because "we have so much in common", this does not mean we will love and delight in each other.

Delighting in One's Partner

Naturally there cannot be real love if there is no delight in one's partner. Real loving partners will delight in each other no matter whether they are similar, different, complementary, non-complementary, on the same page, or not, etc. etc.

Developing beyond two years of age and up to young adulthood involves a process of incredible complexity — of emotions, experiences, skills, encounters, relationships and so on. As I said earlier, two people who are such very complex "objects" simply cannot easily and spontaneously fit together so that they delight in a snug "yin-yang" type perfect bond. Such a yin-yang image melts down two incredibly complex real mutlti-dimensional objects to two flat, two-dimensional unreal, abstract concepts, creating an ideal image that has totally wiped out the complex reality of the situation.

What creates the most delightful adult couple's relationships? When the partners have much in common? But what does that mean? That they are the same? She likes jogging; he likes jogging. It can also mean that their differences complement each other. He is a musician; she is a dancer or singer. She is very serious; he makes her laugh. She likes socialising; he likes doing the background work which involves being alone and concentrating on practicalities that need attending to. And so on.

Some people want to find partners which are very similar to them. Having "something in common" means having many of the same interests, values, beliefs. Others are happy with complementary things: she is logical and scientific; he is a poet and writer. Yet what each does somehow inspires and stimulates the work of the other. They love each other because they complement each other. Some of the great love stories presented to us in the movies or other media are often of this sort. But sometimes we need to be sceptical of those . . .

The mother-infant relationship is also one of complementariness. Two "differences" get together and create a unique magical bond. She is "Big"; he is "Small". Perhaps the baby, especially in the earliest phases "thinks" about mum and himself as "we are the same, you and I". The great love stories about complementary couples might very well be recreations of mother-child bonds.

I would like to suggest that all these "formulae for a delighting and delightful relationship" are totally meaningless. Two people who are the same might not necessarily delight in each other. They might hate each other. Such a married couple, this author wickedly imagines, will divorce on the grounds of "incompatible similarities".

Neither do a couple who clearly complement each other in some areas necessarily have deep delight, and/or erotic feelings for each other.

This is not to say that a couple who are very much "the same" cannot totally delight in that sameness, being "on the same page in so many areas". And a couple who are different from each other, but complement each other very well, may very well benefit from and delight in their complementarity.

But a couple who are not the same in any way might still totally delight in their differences. And a couple who have differences which in no way complement each other can still totally delight in each other.

I would also like to suggest that to talk of any couple as being just one of these kinds is inevitably over-generalisation. Imagine that the following applies to you and your partner: You have many things in common: similar interests, values, beliefs, etc. You might love the sameness or be indifferent to them, or even dislike them intensely.

You will also have areas where you complement each other. In this you are a good team. But that does not guarantee that you love the situation. You might resent it, not quite want it —or be totally indifferent to it, neutral to it.

Also, you will have areas where about which you have nothing in common, are not the same, and have no qualities complementing each other, and yet might totally delight in those areas with one another.

I *do* tend to think that <u>the highest forms</u> of intimate relationship is where a couple's complementarity means they mutually stimulate and seed each other: what one does sparks creativity and life in the other. Such a couple co-creates things (makes metaphorical "babies" out of what each contributes.) But this does not rule out <u>adequate</u> relationships where each partner has his or her own area of creativity unrelated to the other – as long as they delight in each other and have areas of enjoyment being together.

As adults, we need to see that our adult activities, and skills make a difference to the world.
Insofar as I am infantile, I want to feel that my passivity, and lack of skill and development, makes a difference.
I want "unconditional love" without having to do anything for it.

This book has suggested that the popular Soul Mate idea for a perfect relationship is in essence a regressive state that needs to be outgrown. All the same, if there is indeed an adult and mature side to the seeking of a well-bonded "Soul Mate" (i.e. the best possible relationship you can have with someone) it might be this: that I am seeking a relationship with someone with whom I can express the deepest, widest, highest part of myself. But often, in New Age writings on this topic, the suggestion is that the Soul Mate will *bring* you "soul", not that you have to "find soul in *yourself* first" and bring *that* into a soulful relationship. Take this clip from an Australian Natural Health Magazine:

> ... *Soul Mates provide feelings of stability, intimacy, a sense of purpose, security, love, sexual attraction, a desire to have children, but at the same time can arouse feelings of vulnerability and fear.*

As usual, I cannot fail to comment on the "Soul Mate *provides* . . . ", i.e. that you will *get* those things from your Soul Mate. Rather, a feeling of stability, a sense of purpose, feeling secure in yourself, being able to love etc. etc. are all qualities you need to have developed in yourself *before* you will even be ready for a "Soul Mate" – by which I mean a good partner.

I repeat: You need to *bring* those "soulful" things to a relationship, not expect to *find* them there, ready-made.

We must first find love *inside* ourselves, find our ability to love, and will thereby be less vulnerable.

Only now we can seek to truly connect with another *who has done the same*.

Expressing The Deepest, Widest, Highest Part Of Myself

As adults, we need to see that our adult <u>activities, and skills</u> make a difference to the world. We want some of our best achievements, hard-earned, to affect others and make a difference to their lives.

But insofar as I am infantile, I want to feel that my <u>passivity, and lack of skill and development,</u> makes a difference. I want "unconditional love" *without having to do anything for it.*

By bringing an independent, strong me to a relationship, part of my actualisation as a relationship partner is activated. A worthy partner takes my growth and actualisation as a challenge to theirs, and to our growth together as a couple.

That is to say, in real love what makes an excellent partner *is an ability to meet the adult,* developed and developing *you* — to be touched by the significance of it, to appreciate its value, and to respond meaningfully to it, even if just by listening and understanding.

And to the extent that you may be regressed and undeveloped, real love provides you with the space to change this – *if* you are aware of the regression, cognizant of the need to change, and willing to do the necessary emotional work.

However, real love does not validate the regressiveness as a meaningful and final way to be!

The best relationship is the one where your actualisation of yourself, by yourself, for yourself, is delighted in and appreciated by your partner. But if your actualisation of yourself is heavily dependent upon your partner's giving you delight and appreciation and encouragement for your development, then you are regressed.

In a grownup relationship you have matured enough to know what you are, who you are, and who you are developing into. You appreciate and validate all this in yourself, by yourself, for yourself.

The appreciation and delight in this from your partner (and indeed from others) is just a cherry on the cake of your own self appreciation.

Actualising Our Potentials — Our Visions For Our Future

I have concentrated, as many theorists do, on our pasts, on how childhood affects adult intimacy. The modern "scientific" mind is geared to looking for "causes", which are things which happen before "effects". How did my past create, cause the present state of my intimate relationship? It's a *hark-back theory*. What is the "unfinished business" from my past?

But human consciousness creates drives in us by setting up visions of possible futures. We have "unfinished business" about our futures too, about fulfilling our dreams. We have "purposes" we want to fulfil, projects we want to complete (even of the emotional kind). So we need a *"hark-forward" theory* too.

That is, we need a vision of the possible potentials of our relationship, potentials we may be far from even realizing right now. We could call this the potential area.

> The un-sexy can become more sexy; the less educated can become more educated; those who can't dance can learn to dance, or sing, or paint, or play a musical instrument, or become good or fit at a sport, and so on and so forth.

What is meant here is that there are many things that do not at first exist in a relationship that can develop later. The un-sexy can become more sexy; the less educated can become more educated; those who can't dance can learn to dance, or sing, or paint, or play a musical instrument, or become good or fit at a sport, and so on and so forth.

In fact, our human potential is always prodding us to become more than what we currently are, and in intimate relationships, it means becoming a richer and more effective partner to one's partner.

Mature love not only confronts the past, created, ready-made reality of a relationship but also has a vision of what potentially can be made of this relationship, of what "cakes" can be "baked" with these ingredients, of the alchemy capable of altering the "chemistry" of the relationship.

So a mature lover knows not only what is real in this relationship, but what is ideal, or at least, what is possible in the direction of the ideal. And the mature lover knows what to do to move the relationship in that direction.

In this relationship, how do we actualize "us"? What is our identity as a couple?

This is a vision of the possibilities of the relationship that goes beyond just the healing of wounds and the resolving of conflicts. And it certainly goes beyond the idealized notion of romantic love that is projected from the pains and joys of childhood. And it goes beyond the spontaneously occurring positive aspects that are already existent in a relationship.

It goes to that which can be *co-created* by this couple, actualizing the potential of their identity. In this connection, I think Maslow's concept of "*self*-actualisation" should be extended to a concept of "*us*-actualisation" or "*couple*-actualisation". In this relationship, how do we actualise "us"? What is our identity as a couple?

I think that we can talk of two types of this kind of actualisation.

The adult in us can conceive of, have a definite concept of future possibilities we might seek to fulfil in our lives. One expression of this is pre-marriage counselling that challenges a couple to examine their current values and how they want to actualise them in the future. Actually, I think all and any couples planning on creating a future together can do well to discuss what their current dreams for the future are, and the values on which those dreams are based.

And then there is "soul" — from the land of the great knowing unknown, from the invisible, silent world, potential futures might show themselves about which we simply had no idea, and which we will have to deal with as they arise. Dealt with creatively, they add to the unique history of us as a couple, and can enhance our love. ("Soul" is the subject of a chapter in *Falling for Love,* where this concept is expanded upon.)

Long ago I wrote these lines and pasted them on my mirror:

> *Some of our dreams are meant to be broken,*
> *to make way for other dreams*
> *which are meant to come true.*

But to the extent that we can think about, plan and launch ourselves as a couple into the future we now think we want, it is worth sharing our dreams, plans, projects, and especially our values — what we value as important goals to strive toward, and how, and with what morality we shall do so.

112

> **Some of our dreams are meant to be broken, to make way for other dreams which are meant to come true.**

In deciding to try and make it with someone, we should not only look at what is spontaneously and obviously occurring, but what potentials there are for our future. Thus we need to *talk* about our dreams, our hopes, but especially our values, about what we really have energy for actualising in the future.

Whether we are going somewhere together or going on separate paths together, it is worth imagining the future together and evaluating whether we will delight in each other's future direction, or perhaps be disappointed or uninterested or even disgusted by it.

Thus we need to look not just at our current, discovered best fit, as it occurs spontaneously in the romantic period, because that is almost certain to contain a highly limited amount of information about each other.

We need to know each other's visions *beyond the romantic period* if we are to have any hope of making decisions for commitment we are happy with.

It is finding a *perfect-enough* meshing of our lifestyles.

TRUE LOVE, IN CONCLUSION

At the least, True Love should contain both truth and love.

Truth often brings up things that are less than delightful, things we don't necessarily feel like being supportive of. But those harsh truths need to be handled, their power dampened, their spirits transformed. And this takes skill and compassion.

Because it is often truth which splits relationships apart, we need to learn how to be excellent containers capable of holding truth *with* love, understanding and compassion. We need to be the solid jar that can hold the brewing liquid pressurizing within and not crack up.

And sometimes the truth that arises is simply saying: here is an area where you have to grow up. Or here is an area where you sincerely need to learn how to deal with this conflict.

And ultimately, we have to *make* love, not *find* it. Well, let us say rather that, after we have *found* love, we will not be excused from having to *make* love, hence to learn the art and science and skills and realisations that develop us into better lovers.

113

Having found the most unique partner possible for us will not release us from learning the lessons and skills and ways of being better at relationships, at sustaining existing love, at making new love.

The perfect-fit areas of love where we can simply discover love and delight (assuming we are seeing as clearly as possible) are different from the imperfect-fit areas, where we have to *make* love, to create it where it might not initially exist spontaneously.

This means that we have to learn to *make* love, have it as an ability, both within intimate relationships, and without, in relation to all people generally. As Erich Fromm suggested in his book *The Art of Loving* — we have to develop love as an art. That is, we have to learn the skill, the ability to love. He suggested that the learning of any art requires patience, discipline, and, above all, that the learning of the art of love must be seen as one of the highest values in one's life.

But if love were only a skill, only an art which we carry into the world, then theoretically we could form an intimate connection, perhaps a marriage, with almost anyone. But clearly, we do seek some sort of uniqueness in our bond, something that is special about the two people who are us, that sparks delight more than if either of us were with any of a whole load of other people all around us.

In Otto Preminger's 1954 movie *Carmen Jones* (an all-Black, American take of Bizet's opera *Carmen*, with English words) the lead was played by Dorothy Dandridge, the first black actress to be nominated for an Academy Award. She sings:

Love's a baby, dat grows up wild,

and he won't do what you want him to.

Love ain't nobody's angel child,

And he won't pay any mind to you

It's true that if love is indeed "a baby that grows up wild", then it makes sense that the wild spontaneous mad delight of regressive love can take you on a rollercoaster that goes its own way at its own speed and "pays no mind to you".

For this reason, it is important that, for the sake of real and adult love, both you and your partner need to grow beyond feelings which are simply infantile recreations.

A true, real intimate bond formed by grownup, adult qualities in two complex, developed people is a many-sided (multi-valent) bond rich in possibilities for continuous development towards ever-deepening intimacy, wisdom and satisfaction.

But this requires more than just that we *fall* in love.

It requires that we learn to *stand* in love, *walk* in love, *run and jump* in love.

In ending, I wish you love — a love that you will not just *fall for*, but *arise from*, so you can truly come to say you are *standing in love*.

And from there, perhaps proceed to walking in love, then running in love, and even perhaps, at last, *flying* in real love.

End of Grownup Love

—   *Aron Gersh*
London
September 2018

THE END

ADDENDUM

THE FAMOUS RICHARD BACH/LESLIE PARISH SOUL MATE RELATIONSHIP

Richard Bach is the famous author of the multimillion bestselling book *Jonathan Livingstone Seagull*.

In his later book, *A Bridge Across Forever*, he describes his constant search for, and eventual finding, of his Soul Mate. Leslie Parish was already a famous American actress, who was working for a publishing company helping Bach with the marketing and sales of his books. They fell in love, declared to the world they were Soul Mates, wrote a book called *"One"*, and toured America, lecturing. Bach told his audiences there was no question about Soul Mates the two of them could not answer. Their "forever" relationship lasted about 20 years, then they divorced. During one of their public appearances when married, Leslie Parish made the following quote (below) as to what the meaning of a Soul Mate is. I want to analyse this quote in terms of the ideas I have expressed about the elements of regression which I described in this book. I know too little about this pair personally and do not wish to make any judgments or observations about their actual real life relationship, or about their breakup. The only reality I am concerned about is that their "forever" relationship did not quite last "forever", an undeniable fact . . . but so what, some might say. Here is the famous quote:

THAT RICHARD BACH/LESLIE PARISH QUOTE

"A Soul Mate is someone who has locks that fit our keys, and keys to fit our locks. When we feel safe enough to open the locks, our truest selves step out, and we can be completely and honestly who we are; we can be loved for who we are and not for who we're pretending to be. Each unveils the best part of the other.
No matter what else goes wrong around us, with that one person, we're safe in our own paradise.
Our Soul Mate is someone who shares our deepest longings, our sense of direction. When we're two balloons, and together our direction is up, chances are we've found the right person . . . "

Okay, I said that, I would analyse that famous quote on what is a Soul Mate, from the point of view of my "elements of regression". Well, for one thing, much (not all) of the quote is couched in terms of me as recipient fulfilling my needs with you as giver. Is there a hidden narcissism here? Although they mean

116

to suggest that the forces of giving work both ways, it is interesting what happens when we rewrite some of the sentences from the point of view of someone who wants to *give* love rather than receive it. (And please note, I am talking here about true giving, giving-to-give, not giving-to-get.)

For example:

> **When we feel safe enough to open the locks, our truest selves step out,   and we can be completely and honestly who we are; we can be loved for who we are and not for who we're pretending to be.**

BECOMES

When we make <u>our partners</u> feel safe enough to have <u>their</u> locks opened, <u>their</u> truest selves will step out, and <u>they</u> will be completely and honestly who <u>they</u> are; they can be loved for who <u>they</u> are, and not for what <u>they</u> are   pretending to be.

And

> **No matter what else goes wrong around us, with that one   person, we're safe in our own paradise.**

BECOMES

No matter what else goes wrong around <u>my partner</u>, with <u>me</u>, <u>he or she is</u> safe in our own paradise.

And

> **Our Soul Mate is someone who shares our deepest longings, our sense of   direction.**

BECOMES

As your Soul Mate, I share your deepest longings, your sense of   direction.

I wonder how it sounds to you, dear Reader, when you re-couch the Soul Mate needs from the passive recipient point of view and decide to make yourself the *provider* in a Soul Mate relationship — to *give* what the other needs, as much as or more than *getting* what *you* need.

Of course, I know that Bach and Parish meant the quote to apply equally to both partners. But each can be equally narcissistic, expecting equally to be the recipients of need-fulfilment (and not the responsible providers). And what is more, expecting that process to happen spontaneously, magically, without the need for any development of relationship skill, to be able to get beyond one's own neediness and to be able to provide genuine love and support in a relationship.

DEPENDENCE

I can't say I feel sure that any of what I wrote about *Dependence* applies particularly to the quote we are dealing with. The following line is the only one I find potentially relevant.

> *No matter what else goes wrong around us, with that one person, we're safe in our own paradise.*

I tend to read that more as "No matter what they say about me, or do to me, you keep me safe, you are my paradisical place of safety". In other words, without you, I cannot feel safe inside myself. And note that earlier I pointed out how good we feel, how strong and independent, when our needs are totally fulfilled by the people we are actually totally dependent on *in order* to feel such confidence and independence.

In terms of their real lives, rather than the Soul Mate quote, my guess is that Bach and Parish are both very BIG people. It is easy to see how, in different areas of their lives, each could be BIG to the other's small.

Hence the difficulty of seeing the dependence in them would have come from both processes: the mutuality of the dependence, as well as the fact of them each satisfying an area of "Small's" need, making "small" not feel small at all.

A SENSE OF BOUNDARILESSNESS

Leslie Parish once said in an interview, at the beginning of their great Soul Mate relationship, something like, "We don't know where the one of us begins and the other ends". A journalist in the audience wrote that she immediately saw this as problematic.

> *Our Soul Mate is someone who shares our deepest longings, our sense of direction. When we're two balloons, and together our direction is up, chances are we've found the right person.*

In this quote there is an implicit assumption that a solid "Soul Mate" loving bond cannot be created by two people who have different "deepest longings" for what they want to do, experience, or achieve in their lives. But why not? If each has a deep appreciation, respect, and support for the other's longings, why *can't* they be the "right person" for each other? Why do they have to be *the same*?

In the womb, there is, for the most part, no boundary between the blood flow of the foetus and that of the mother, no "separation", no barrier. Verbally, mother and foetus might say: "We share the same things, equally, together".

After birth, in the first few months, this sense continues psychologically. "We are not separate. In what we want from life, we are the same. Because of this, our union is perfect."

So often in the social space I see how people (including myself), when they want to bond with someone they have newly met, make suggestions about how "we are the same", or "I too feel that" etc. etc. There seems to be a primitive sense in us all that *in order to bond we have to be "the same"*. That seems to be a "default" position.

I like the modern word "default", from the computer world. A "default" choice is pre-chosen for us, as it is considered to be the most likely one, the most popular one. For this, you just have to hit the easy-to-find, big "Return" button on your keyboard. But if you have to stop and think, and make a more considered choice from a list of other possibilities, you need more disciplined action, more refined and subtler movements.

I think that the choice to be different, to disagree, the choice to suggest that "we are not the same", but we can *still* be bonded, be friends – I think that this choice goes beyond the easy primitive "default" state of "we need to be the *same* to feel bonded, part of the *same* group or tribe".

So, to return to the quote: two balloons are very similar, and going in the same direction adds to their sameness. But in the complex *real* world, there is not just up and down, but a thousand directions and more that someone can take.

The "mature image" of bonding I spoke of earlier (adult/adult instead of mother/child) is of two very different adults, who have well-developed boundaries which they maintain when they bond with someone. The easy, archetypal image, as I said, is a mature male and mature female bonding by sexual intercourse and creating a baby. It happens best when each has grown fully independent of their own parents. And it happens best because each is different and maintains that difference.

"We complement each other" is a statement meaning: "although we are different, our differences enhance each other". I am not suggesting that Bach and Parish did not live up to this mature form of connecting. As I said, without knowing them, I can't comment on their relationship. I am simply saying that the quote expresses a regressive, immature way of creating a "beautiful blissful bond" — notably by being *clones* of each other, and each going exactly where the other is going. We don't know who is leading and who is following.   In free-style dancing, that is a lovely state to reach — two people working on a fabulous harmony with each other. But here two separate individuals start off with their own particular rhythms, paces, moves, etc., and slowly match them to each other.

A bond of two very different people who are *not* the same, and are *not* going *spontaneously* in the same direction – *that* is where *real* love is finally created.

On the other hand, I must give Bach and Parish full marks for their "letting go" process when the partners' life processes together were over, and it was time to move on. No recriminations towards each other for having different needs at that time of their lives, no anger at the other for changing direction, choosing other paths.

But no marks, from this author at least, for not admitting mistakes, for not bothering to rephrase and refine what they previously preached. Once, they said there was no question about finding a Soul Mate that they could not answer! Would they still say that today?

**End of the
Richard Bach/Leslie Parish quote
chapter**

AFTER MATTERS

FOOTNOTES

101

One, by the way, was the title of the Richard Bach book written with his Soul Mate Leslie Parish, after they married. He had just published *A Bridge Across Forever*, which was about him finding her, his Soul Mate, and they entered into a "forever" marriage which lasted 20 years before divorce. Bach became famous for his first book *Jonathan Livingstone Seagull*. There will be a chapter on this in *Aspects of Love*.

130

Written in 1982 by Jeff Silbar and Larry Henley. Bette Midler made it famous in 1988

132

This author recently saw a TV program called Kinky Britain, about bondage in the dominant-submissive sexual act. The hidden interviewer was curious about whether these people had very dominating mothers, and apparently, in all cases, the answer was a very distinct "No!". That was not the point for me, whether in *post infancy childhood* one had a domineering mother or not. The reality, far more primal, goes back in time to those early years — for the baby, mother is emotionally and factually enormous, and the baby's vulnerability is correspondingly emotionally and factually enormous, making it feel incredibly small. This is precisely what is being regressed to in these adult forms of kinky sexuality! Vulnerable *infantile* sexuality is being recreated in adulthood!

133

Freud's notion of this Oedipal rivalry referred to children of about three to five years of age. I would think it happens in the infant stage already (i.e. roughly the first two years of life). At any rate, the focus of this book has been on the very early dyadic bond between baby and mother, and I have purposely not expounded on the effects of the later stages after infancy, which involve triads more and more, sibling rivalry, and so on.

137

Sorry, dear reader. I can't find where I got this quote from. I only know that it was from a real interview with a real criminal, not a piece of fiction. As I remember, the interview was in a prison.

152

As far as I know, in knightly times the yearning by a knight for a princess he was jousting for would in principle be unfulfillable — nevertheless, the deep yearning seems to have been validated as meaningful.

155

See Wikipedia.org, under the heading "Richard Burton"

131

Yinyang. (2012). Encyclopædia Britannica. Encyclopædia Britannica Ultimate Reference Suite. Chicago: Encyclopædia Britannica.

157

I unfortunately was not granted the permission to publish the original lines from that song.

191

I wrote copiously in Falling For Love about why I disagreed with Carl Jung's notion that childhood processes like "childlike innocence" and "basic trust" and "playfulness" and so on are important to recapture in adult life. Not that I think they are not important. But I was saying that the value of their appearance in adult life depends fully on the full picture, the total context. with a person who has a wonderful childlike playfulness might seem ecstatic at first, but if the percentage of that playfulness is too much, and the percentage of adult responsibility is too little, then that wonderful childlike playfulness will be rather dysfunctional to the whole picture.

BOOK REFERENCES IN
THE SOUL MATE ILLUSION

One of the Family — 40 years with the Krays

21 April 2016 (reprint
by Maureen Flanagan
Publisher: Arrow

Frances Kray — the Tragic Bride

3 Sept. 2015 (revised edition)
by Jacky Hyams
Publisher: John Blake Publishing Ltd

The Art of Loving

(Classics of Personal Development)
Paperback
7 Oct 1995
by Erich Fromm (Author)
Publisher: Thorsons; New Ed edition
First published in Great Britain by
George Allen & Unwin, 1957

The Universe is a Green Dragon

1 June 1984
by Brian Schwimme
Publisher: Bear & Company;
Original ed. edition (1 Jun. 1984)

BIBLIOGRAPHY

Relevant both to

THE SOUL MATE ILLUSION

and to

FALLING FOR LOVE

Playing and Reality
13/5/1971 (original version)
By Donald Winnicott
Hard Copy
(Later editions available aplenty)

101 Romantic Ideas,
Michael Webb,
Kindle Edition available from Amazon.

Adultery
1 Aug 2014
Paul Coelho
Publisher: Vintage Books

Transactional Analysis in Psychotherapy: The Classical Handbook to its Principles
28 Feb 2001
by Eric Berne
Condor Books

Other Books by Eric Berne
Games People Play: The Psychology of Human Relationships (Penguin Life)
2 Jun 2016
by Eric Berne
Publisher: Penguin Life

What Do You Say After You Say Hello
30 Apr 1975
by Eric Berne
Publisher: Corgi; New Ed edition

Sex in Human Loving
27 Sep 1973
by Eric Berne
Publisher: Penguin Books Ltd; New edition edition

See Also:
I'm Ok, You're Ok
5 Jan 2012
by Thomas A. Harris
Publisher: Arrow

Warriors of the Heart
16 Dec 2009
Danaan Parry
Publisher: BookSurge Publishing

Getting The Love You Want: A Guide for Couples
3 Jan 2005
Harville Hendrix
Paperback
Publisher: Simon & Schuster UK; New Ed edition
Originally published in 1988,

Amazon.com comments on this book as follows:
"GETTING THE LOVE YOU WANT
has helped thousands of couples attain more loving, supportive and deeply satisfying relationships. In this groundbreaking book, Dr Harville Hendrix shares with you what he has learned about the psychology of love during more than thirty years of working as a therapist and helps you transform your relationship into a lasting source of love and companionship. For this edition of his classic book, Dr Hendrix and his wife, Helen LaKelly Hunt, have added a new introduction describing the powerful influence this book has had on so many people over the years. With its step-by-step programme, GETTING THE LOVE YOU WANT will help you create a loving, supportive and revitalized partnership."

Making Marriage Simple
—Ten Truths for Changing the Relationship You Have into the
One You Want
April 2014
Harville Hendrix
Paperback
Publisher: Harmony; Reprint edition

Also by Harville Hendrix

Keeping the Love You Find: Guide for Singles
6 Feb 1995
by Harville Hendrix
Paperback
Publisher: Pocket Books; New edition edition

NonViolent Communication
— A Language of Compassion
January 2001 (5th printing)
By Marshall Rosenberg
Paperback
Publisher: PuddleDancer Press

The Heart of Love: How to Go Beyond Fantasy to Find True
Relationship Fulfilment
15 Jan 2007
by Dr. John F. Demartini

Publisher: Hay House

Radical Honesty, the New Revised Edition: How to Transform
Your Life by Telling the Truth
15 May 2005
by Brad Blanton
Publisher: Sparrowhawk Publishing; Revised edition

A Doll's House
11 May 2010
by Henrik Ibsen
Paperback: 136 pages
Publisher: Longman (28 Aug. 2008)

Childhood And Society
20 Apr 1995
by E H Erikson
Publisher: Vintage; New Edition
Originally published 1950

Erik Erikson first published his eight-stage theory of human development in his 1950 book *Childhood and Society*.
The chapter outlining the model was entitled *'The Eight Ages of Man'*.
He expanded and refined his theory in later books and revisions, notably:
Identity and the Life Cycle (1959);
Insight and Responsibility (1964);
The Life Cycle Completed: A Review (1982, revised 1996 by Joan Erikson);
and *Vital Involvement in Old Age* (1989).

The 5 Love Languages
Paperback
20 Feb 2015
by Gary Chapman (Author)
Publisher: Moody Press; First edition

The Little Prince
29 Oct 2001
By St.Antoine de Exupery & Katherine Woods
Published by: Egmont

The Course in Miracles
21 May 2008
By Foundation of Inner Peace

Published by: Foundation for Inner Peace

Soul Mates
Honouring the Mysteries of Love and Relationship
30 April 1994
by Thomas Moore
Publisher: Element Books; Paperback/softback edition

Care of the Soul
How to add depth and meaning to everyday life
1996
by Thomas Moore
Publisher: Piatkus

The Eden Project: In Search of the Magical Other - Jungian Perspective on Relationship
12 August 1998
By James Hollis
Publisher: Inner City Books

Client-Centered Therapy
1951
 By Carl Rogers
Cambridge, Massachussets
The Riverside Press

The Future of Humanistic Psychology
2 Sept 2013
 By Richard House (author), David Kalisch (editor) and Jennifer Maidman.   (quote inside by John Heron)
Publisher: PCCS Books; 1st edition

The Original Warm Fuzzy Tale
30 April 1994
by Claude Steiner
Publisher: Jalmar Press Inc.,U.S. (Dec. 1985)

Motivation and Personality
1954
by Abraham Maslow
Publisher: Pearson; 3rd edition (7 Jan. 1997)

The Best American Poetry
22 Sept. 2009
by David Wagoner & David Lehman (Editors)
Publisher: Scribner Book Company

Knots
1 April 1970
by R.D. Laing
Publisher: Routledge

Why Marriages Succeed or Fail — and how you can make yours last
11 December 2002
by John Gottman Ph.D
Publisher: Simon & Schuster

Love and Will
7 March, 2011
by Rollo May
Publisher: W. W. Norton & Company; Reprint edition

Well, that's me with my favourite summer cotton shirt.

I worked as a Humanistic Psychotherapist in London for about eight years, then ran a small Humanistic Psychology magazine for seven years, as editor, and almost everything else, which is what one does on small magazines run for love. It was called *Human Potential* magazine.

My studies: I achieved my bachelor's degree in psychology from Witwatersrand University in Johannesburg, South Africa, and then my Honours degree at UNISA there. In London I did my Masters degree at Antioch University (an American University based in Yellow Springs, Ohio) when they were operating in London for about 10 years. I also trained and worked as a psychotherapist there.

Currently I am semi-retired and am trying to study to understand some of the things I never got to understand in a lifetime in psychology. I do a lot of my own thinking, and try to think things through as thoroughly as I can, constantly challenging myself as to how any particular idea might be wrong, might be an illusion. I am a "righter" — one who tries to right the wrongs of his own writing! I also "walk my talk" to the highest of my ability. There is nothing I suggest in the book that I am not capable of myself, and am prepared to be challenged on that.

I do want to honour the handful of women I have had deep, intimate connections with in my life. Each one has given me so much, taught me so much, and I cannot help but refer you, dear reader to the Thomas Moore long "boxed" quote in *Falling for Love* about honouring all those who have touched our lives deeply along the rocky road to love. Though I have totally trashed here the concept of "Soul Mates" as it is generally used in western society (i.e. as the spontaneous, perfect fit) some of my past relationships have carried on as more than just friendships – why, almost as a feeling that we are "soul friends" forever! I am not allowed to talk about my current relationship situation. No! It's not what you think! No! It's not that either! I present you with this vague stimulus, and you may project your imagination onto it (see the writings on "projection" herein). Here's encouraging the growth of love in you and yours, and thanks for reading . . . all the way to here!

Aron Gersh
London
September 2018

www.ingramcontent.com/pod-product-compliance
Lightning Source LLC
Chambersburg PA
CBHW021129020426
42331CB00005B/691